CAUTION:
Sexual Choices May Be Hazardous To Your Health

CAUTION: Sexual Choices May Be Hazardous To Your Health

EVERYTHING YOU NEED TO KNOW

MARY ANN MAYO

Zondervan Publishing House
Grand Rapids, Michigan

CAUTION: SEXUAL CHOICES MAY BE HAZARDOUS TO YOUR HEALTH
Copyright © 1989 by Mary Ann Mayo

Published by the Zondervan Publishing House
1415 Lake Drive, S.E., Grand Rapids, Michigan 49506

Library of Congress Cataloging-in-Publication Data

Mayo, Mary Ann
    Caution : sexual choices may be hazardous to your health :
everything you need to know / Mary Ann Mayo.
      p. cm.
    "Youth books."
    Summary: Advice with a Christian viewpoint for teenagers exploring
decisions about sexual behavior. Includes four plot-your-own stories
about teenagers with choices to make.
     1. Sexual ethics for teenagers—juvenile literature. [1. Sexual ethics. 2. Plot-
your-own stories.] I. Title. II. Title: Caution, sexual choices may be hazardous to your
health.
  HQ35.M369   1989
  176–dc20   89–22565
                                             CIP
                                             AC

ISBN 0-310-44261-3

Edited by David Lambert and Joyce Ellis
Designed by Ann Cherryman

Printed in the United States of America

89 90 91 92 93 94 / PP / 10 9 8 7 6 5 4 3 2 1

CONTENTS

HOW TO USE
THIS BOOK

Please— don't try to read this book from beginning to end. But do read pages 11 to 18. On those pages, you'll read the stories of four teenagers; some of them will be like you, and some won't. There are six ways for each of those stories to end. The choices those teenagers make will determine how their lives will turn out—just like in real life. Of course, in this book, *you'll* be asked to make those choices for them, just as you make similar choices for yourself every day. And those choices—in this book, and in life—may lead to success or disaster!

When you make a choice for one of those four characters, you'll be given instructions to turn to another page to continue the story; you'll be given a symbol and sometimes a number to look for on that page. Follow those instructions to see what happens next. If, after you've finished one of the stories, you want to see what might have happened if you'd made different choices, just go back to the beginning or back to a previous choice point and follow the instructions to a different conclusion.

At a few places in each story, I'll take "time out" to give you some information that directly affects the choice you're about to make for the character you're reading about—information about birth control, or divorce, or masturbation, or breaking up, or marriage, or guilt, or pornography, or many other things. *Please take a minute to read that information.* We *can* make wise sexual choices in life—but there are things we need to know first.

Have fun! And remember—

CAUTION: SEXUAL CHOICES MAY BE HAZARDOUS TO YOUR HEALTH!

RED FLAG!

FOR THOSE WHO HAVE NO SPIRIT OF ADVENTURE—OR ARE SUPPOSED TO BE STUDYING FOR A SPANISH TEST INSTEAD OF READING A SEX BOOK—OR WHO NEED INFORMATION FAST. IF YOU WANT TO KNOW ABOUT:

JENNIFER'S STORY

As Jennifer sat in the sunny courtyard at school, finishing the last bite of her sandwich, she heard her name and looked up.

"Jennifer! Jennifer!" Doreen called. "You made it!"

Jennifer grinned at the sight of her overweight friend running across the lawn, waving a paper in the air. The anticipation was over.

Several other friends crowded around. "Congratulations, Jen! That's great!"

"A-a-all ri-i-ight!" Bill tossed his math book in the air for emphasis.

"Only one year at this school, and you make the cheerleading squad as a senior," another said in mock envy.

Still huffing and puffing, Doreen caught up with the crowd. "Are you going to tell Jeff right away?" she asked her friend.

"I can't," Jennifer replied, hardly able to wait. After all the pain of the previous year's move, leaving friends, and being the "new kid," now her wildest dream had come true. And she couldn't tell Jeff right away. "He has a college interview this afternoon," she told her friends. "But he thought he'd be home shortly after school let out. I'll call him as soon as I get home. Maybe Mom will let us celebrate down at TCBY tonight."

There was no one she would rather celebrate with. Meeting Jeff had turned her disastrous year around. She was sure she loved him. Her mind strayed from the well-wishers to an image of Jeff, holding her tightly and spinning her around in pure joy. She could feel his arms around her and tingled at the thought of her body next to his.

"Earth to Jennifer, earth to Jennifer," interrupted Doreen. "I'll bet I know where your mind was."

Jennifer wondered if it were really that obvious. Lately, she had felt as though she wouldn't mind if Jeff wanted to "go all the way" with her. . .

What Will Jennifer Choose?

■ Jennifer decides her feeling for Jeff is the real thing. She is in love.
GO TO PAGE 19 AND LOOK FOR ■

✱✱ Jeff didn't try anything on their date that night, but Jennifer was so turned on when she got home that she began masturbating in the bathroom to relieve her sexual tension.
GO TO PAGE 45 AND LOOK FOR ✱✱

○ Jennifer concludes that since things "feel so right" between them, she and Jeff must be right for each other. She encourages his advances on their date that night, and they have sexual intercourse.
GO TO PAGE 71 AND LOOK FOR ○

TO MAKE SURE YOU'RE FOLLOWING THE CORRECT STORY, LOOK FOR THE SYMBOL, NAME, AND SOMETIMES A NUMBER.

JASON'S STORY

While Jason walked home from football practice, his mind kept running through the new play the coach had just taught them. He didn't hear anyone behind him.

"Yo, Jason," Bob called, catching up with him.

Jason turned and eyed the smooth, black-leather-jacket-clad senior the girls called "The Hunk." Jason kept walking. "Whatcha doin' Bob, slummin'?" he asked, picking up the pace. Jason's house was just down the street.

"Nah, I was just scouting the neighborhood," Bob replied. 'I heard that easy new girl moved in somewhere around here." The way he rolled his eyes, he didn't have to say anything more.

"You must mean Carly." Jason smirked. "She's a turn-on, all right. She's in my English class, and with all her jiggling and wiggling I can hardly keep my mind on nouns and verbs and all that good stuff!" They both laughed.

Bob was suddenly serious. "Who's going to win the game Friday? Do you think Dan's being out will hurt the team?"

"No," Jason replied. "We can do it without him." His bravado sounded hollow in his ears. Jason was a so-so player, and if the truth were known, he much preferred his time on the bench to getting creamed on the field. He had discovered, however, that the adage about girls loving men in uniforms was true. And *he* loved the girls. Being an average-looking guy who lived in sexual overdrive most of the time, he took every advantage he could get.

As they reached Jason's driveway, Jason's dad slipped out from under the hood of the car. He was forever adjusting and readjusting something. "Hi, boys."

"Hi, Dad."

"Hi, Mr. Murray."

Wiping his greasy hands on an equally greasy rag, Jason's dad cocked his head. "You fellows been cruising?" he asked playfully. "Find any cute chicks?"

Jason was used to the question. He swung a mock punch at his dad, who returned a few of his own.

Laughing, Jason and Bob invaded the kitchen.

Jason had dated a number of girls and enjoyed playing the field, but sometimes it seemed as if his dad were more concerned about his sex life than he was!

What Will Jason Choose?

■ A friend introduces Jason to Suzy, and somehow she seems different. She always looks nice and is super friendly, but she doesn't wear seductive clothes or make suggestive remarks like a lot of the girls. Jason's friend tells him that Suzy is a Christian. He wants to ask her out.
GO TO PAGE 101 AND LOOK FOR ■

** Jason starts steadily dating Cathy, an attractive girl who seems to know her way around. He knows she likes him, and she has a great body. Her parents aren't as strict as some of the girls he has dated. They give them lots of privacy and free time together, and Jason takes advantage of it.
GO TO PAGE 62 AND LOOK FOR **

○ Jason continues just playing the field. Most of his waking day is spent talking about girls, especially the ones that "do it."
GO TO PAGE 135 AND LOOK FOR ○

TO MAKE SURE YOU'RE FOLLOWING THE CORRECT STORY, LOOK FOR THE SYMBOL, NAME, AND SOMETIMES A NUMBER.

MICHELLE'S STORY

The loudspeaker at the homecoming game blared the score: 14 to 7 in favor of the home team. The stands were packed, and the crowd went wild.

Becky stood at the gate in her usual jeans and KROC-radio sweatshirt and greeted her late-arriving friend. "Michelle, you look great," she said. "Whadja do to your eyes?"

"I just added a little color. Is it too much?" Michelle was worried. Barely thirteen, she hadn't had much experience applying eye shadow.

"No!" Becky said quickly. "It looks great." She hated herself for lying, but Michelle was one of the coolest kids in junior high, and Becky wanted so much to be her friend.

They wormed their way up the stands to what seemed to be the last two seats available. Michelle was delighted to see that there were a couple of good-looking, high-school guys sitting next to them. Becky wasn't so thrilled. Guys made her nervous. When Michelle began to talk to them, Becky suddenly found the "stats" in the program fascinating reading.

"How old are you, Michelle?" one of the boys asked.

"Almost sixteen."

Becky was impressed with how convincing Michelle sounded. *Almost sixteen? Now that took guts,* she thought to herself.

And so a relationship began. Michelle's fully developed body gave Dan, a personable fellow, no reason to suspect how young she was. Within several months their relationship had escalated to include sexual intercourse. And by the time he discovered how young she was, he didn't care. Then Dan graduated and went off to college. Michelle missed him, but some of Dan's friends began asking her out. Her pattern of having sex as part of her relationships continued.

What Will Michelle Choose?

■ Because Michelle has been sexually abused by her father since she was seven years old, she decides that sex is no big deal if it will get the guys to like her.
GO TO PAGE 147 AND LOOK FOR ■

✳✳ Michelle overhears a group of boys talking about how "easy" she is. They joke that she'll "go down" for a stick of gum. The words hurt; she begins to wonder whether she needs to change her behavior to try to salvage her reputation.
GO TO PAGE 78 AND LOOK FOR ✳✳

○ Michelle drops out of school to marry.
GO TO PAGE 163 AND LOOK FOR ○

TO MAKE SURE YOU'RE FOLLOWING THE CORRECT STORY, LOOK FOR THE SYMBOL, NAME, AND SOMETIMES A NUMBER.

ERIC'S STORY

Eric sat down on the locker-room bench and watched the hurried confusion around him as he began to towel-dry his hair.

"Eeyoww! Friday's here," Joe flipped his gym towel at whoever happened to be in range. "Tonight's the night. I've got a date with Cinnnndy!"

Eric sighed. *Man, what's all the fuss about?* he wondered. *Girls are nice, but I don't understand these guys practically worshiping them.*

Joe flipped his towel in Eric's direction. "Whatcha doing tonight, Eric?" he asked.

"Oh, nothin' much." Eric turned his back and began to rummage in his locker for nothing in particular, hoping Joe would lose interest.

"How 'bout doubling with Cindy and me? Her cousin is visiting and needs a date." Joe looked like one of those guys on the cover of *GQ*. To make matters worse, he was friendly, outgoing, and funny. Most everyone liked him.

Eric ended the pretend locker search and slid into his shoes. "No, no thanks," he said quickly.

"Come on. You said you weren't doing anything," Joe insisted.

Stupid! Eric chided himself. *Why didn't I say I had a date, or I'm having a funeral for my pet python, Flex. Anything!* He grabbed his sweats and wadded them into his bag, topping everything off with his wet towel. "I forgot. I promised my mom I'd stay home with the family. She's on one of those family-closeness kicks."

"Well, I think you're just a fag and don't wanna go out with a girl."

Eric swung around, his jaw clenched. He searched Joe's face for some indication that he meant it. But Joe was laughing and had already turned his attention to harassing Bill for his choice of skin pictures on his locker door.

Grabbing his bag, Eric rushed out of the locker room, took the steps three at a time, and headed directly to his car.

Maybe it was true. He sure felt like he didn't fit in with the rest of the guys. Mr. Carter, the P.E. teacher, was more interesting to him than any girl in school. *Fag, fag, fag* . . . The word kept ringing in his ear.

What Will Eric Choose?

■ Eric decides that homosexuality is his fate and his lifestyle.
GO TO PAGE 170 AND LOOK FOR ■

** Eric thinks that maybe he could "cure" himself of his homosexual feelings by finding a girlfriend.
GO TO PAGE 185 AND LOOK FOR **

○ Eric decides to discuss his feelings with his Youth Leader from Campus Life.
GO TO PAGE 191 AND LOOK FOR ○

TO MAKE SURE YOU'RE FOLLOWING THE COR-RECT STORY, LOOK FOR THE SYMBOL, NAME AND SOMETIMES A NUMBER.

LOVE MAKES THE WORLD GO ROUND

Here's what's happening:

JENNIFER: Jennifer has decided that she's in love with Jeff. At least, it feels like love. But is it? Maybe those quiverings in her tummy are left over from the burrito at dinner. Jennifer needs to give some thought to what love is. Does it mean a commitment for life? That's scary! Does it mean "I crave your body"? What is love, anyway?

O1 MICHELLE: Michelle received criticism from some for relinquishing her baby. She understood and accepted that all the options open to her were only second best. She loved April enough, however, to place her in a home that more closely resembled God's plan for healthy child rearing: two parents who love the Lord and have the stability to love and take care of another family member. That option seemed more loving to Michelle than the chance of abuse and neglect the baby might face with a divorced, struggling teen. Was it the loving thing to do?

2 ERIC: Can two homosexuals really be in love? Is their love sufficient to sustain a marriage? Some men Eric meets aren't

interested in love—they're into lust. Eric wants more; he wants a relationship. Will he find it?

Before we continue with these three stories, let's look at some of the things Jennifer, Michelle, and Eric should know about love.

Love Makes the World Go Round

Bumper stickers tell what the owner of the car values or professes to "love": I love my Teddy bear, I love my kids, I love my Doberman, I love God, I love "what's-his-face." Television claims that certain people love mouthwash, underarm deodorant, and 'home-cooked" TV dinners. Just what is love anyway?

Romantic novels, television, and the movies imply that it is a feeling so powerful that we have no choice but to give in to it—the sooner the better. Not to do so, it seems, might result in either mental or physical illness or both!

Brothers and sisters tell us that we will know it when it happens. Our single Aunt Myrtle says it is fleeting, and Mom and Dad insist that anyone under 25 only experiences puppy love.

The problem is, the one English word, *love* , must define a great range of emotions. Eskimos have fifty words for snow. Their livelihood, health, and welfare depends on knowing what kind of snow they will be dealing with. There would be far less confusion in American society if the word *love* had fifty variations. Then everyone would know what everyone else was talking about.

Different words could be used for youthful infatuation with its highly erotic nature, love of food, and love craved to boost self-image.

Interestingly, the original Greek of the New Testament used three different words for love: *agape, phileo,* and *eros.* Although there can be some overlap, each word has its own distinctions. *Agape* describes an unconditional love. This love is expressed even when the person loved isn't acting very lovable. Examples of *agape* love are God's love for us and a mother's love for a child. The basis for marriage should also be *agape* love, a love that continues no matter what trials may come and no matter how unlovable the spouse acts.

Phileo is brotherly love, the love felt for friends. Friends enjoy hanging around together, teasing one another, and being there to listen.

Finally, *eros* love involves passion and bodily arousal. It is the most self-focused of the three.

Adults often tease young people about "puppy love," the most common type of adolescent love. But as someone has said, puppy love feels real to the "puppy." At least in the beginning, it most likely involves a great deal of *eros*. If the relationship has an opportunity to grow, and a couple determines that they like what they have discovered about the personality of the other, a true friendship, *phileo*, results. Eventually, over time, as each individual matures and is capable of placing the needs of the other ahead of his or her own, *agape* love develops.

Christian marriage should involve all three kinds of love. It is *eros* because God made two sexes designed to be attracted to one another and to find mutual joy and contentment in one another's body. It is *phileo* because our design is one of interdependence. A male-female relationship is based on what each sex uniquely brings to the partnership. Christian marriage is *agape* because it is everlasting, like the Lord's covenant to Abraham and then to us.

Few Americans understand arranged marriages just as few Japanese or Indians comprehend the American notion of romantic marriages that last only as long as the feelings do. Healthy marriage is sustained by the trust that springs from commitment. It is strengthened by the genuine respect and friendship of the couple. It is enriched through the intimacy of bodies that were designed to bring pleasure.

Marital love, then, is a special balance of *eros*, *phileo*, and *agape*. But most of the "love" felt in relationships is something short of life-long commitment. The most common love is frequently an intricate balance of *phileo* and *eros* with only a smattering of *agape*. But to be labeled love at all, certain criteria need to be met. The Bible provides a checklist in 1 Corinthians 13. If you want to know whether you're in love, ask yourself:

21

1. Am I patient with him/her?
2. Do I treat him/her with kindness?
3. Am I envious?
4. Do I boast and brag about the relationship or the other's dependence or caring of me?
5. Is the relationship one of pride for me?
6. Are our interactions considerate and uplifting?
7. Am I in this for what I can get, or do I care about what is best for him/her?
8. Do I keep a mental record every time I'm treated unfairly or find my needs not met?
9. Do I play games to assure myself of his/her commitment to me, or do I encourage honesty and truth between us?
10. Am I protective of the relationship and the person, seeking never to place him/her in a compromising or vulnerable position?
11. Is my attitude one of expecting the best from the person and the relationship?
12. Do I tend to give up when the least little thing makes the relationship uncomfortable or difficult?

What happens next?

■ JENNIFER (cont. from page 19)
Jennifer has only seen love defined on television. The tube tells her that if you want to have sex with someone, it probably means you're in love or might be someday, so go for it. Is Jennifer "in like," "in love," or "in lust"? What's in store for her? Choose one for Jennifer:

■1. Jennifer has no one to help her sort through distinctions between the different kinds of love. In her mind she is simply in love, so she continues to nurture her physical arousal. GO TO PAGE 26 AND LOOK FOR ■1

■2. Jennifer goes to a Campus Life meeting and asks her leader about love. She analyzes what she is feeling about Jeff. GO TO PAGE 37 AND LOOK FOR ■2

O1 MICHELLE (cont. from page 19)

Several years later. . .

As Michelle lay in a hospital bed, exhausted from childbirth, she looked up into the concerned blue eyes of her husband, Stan.

Stan beamed. "Our other two have been fed and will stay with Mrs. Clint until I get back," he assured her. "They are so excited and full of questions!" Grabbing one of the straight chairs in the hospital room, he turned it around and straddled it.

Michelle thought he looked like the Cheshire cat in *Alice in Wonderland*. "Thanks for taking such good care of them, Stan," she said weakly. "Are you sure you're not upset that you didn't get your boy?" Though fatigued from a long labor, she needed to talk.

"Are you kidding? I'm delighted!" Stan exclaimed. "This is just the baby for us. Let's face it, Hon. You were born to bring beautiful girls into the world."

Michelle could not reply. Tears choked her throat and streamed down her face.

Stan panicked. Jumping up, he was by her bed in a flash. "Did I say something wrong?"

"I was thinking of April," Michelle finally managed. "Our family is so full of love. She should be with us. She's my little girl, too."

"Michelle, she is with a loving family. And you know what else?"

"What?"

"If you had kept April, we probably would never have met," he reminded her. "And there would be no Barbara, Elizabeth, and now Kathryn."

"I love you, Stan." The tears stopped flowing, but she dabbed at her nose with a tissue. "Hormones!" she cried with a laugh. "God is so faithful. Out of the worst experience of my life have come all these wonderful blessings." She shook her head as in disbelief.

"You've been faithful to the Lord, Michelle," her husband

observed. "Since accepting the Lord as your Savior, you have tried to do his will."

"How can I repay all those people from the teen center who believed in me, encouraged me to go on to school, and prayed for me?"

"The way you live your life is payment," Stan said softly. They hugged one another for a long time.

Michelle continued to be a good mother and wife and to walk in the way of her heavenly Father who loved her unconditionally.

IF YOU WOULD LIKE TO EXPLORE SOME OF THE OTHER CHOICES MICHELLE COULD HAVE MADE, GO TO PAGE 15 OR 169.

■2 ERIC (cont. from page 19)
Eric hung up the phone as Bill walked in.

"Who called?" Bill asked.

"Believe it or not, my folks."

Eric's parents had threatened to break contact forever when he announced his decision to move in with Bill after graduation.

"What did they want?" Bill prodded.

"They invited me to Thanksgiving dinner. But I'm to come alone." Eric threw himself down on the couch, his long legs dangling over the end. He swung his arm over his face in a casual attempt to hide his tears.

"Hey, you should go," Bill said compassionately. "I know you miss them."

"I'm not going without you!" Eric replied through his tears.

Bill finished putting the groceries away and sat on the floor beside Eric with his back against the couch. "I miss my folks too," he said. "If they don't see us together, they can pretend they don't have 'fags' for sons."

Eric sat up and took Bill's hand. "There must be some way to make them understand. It's not like we're out there messing around with everyone. We've got something special."

"We'll never convince them," Bill said.

"I've been thinking about that. What if we got married?"

Bill threw his head back and laughed heartily. "You've got to be kidding."

Eric talked excitedly now. "I'm serious. We have committed ourselves to a monogamous relationship and to a long life together. Let's get married."

Bill slid up onto the couch. "You're serious."

"Perfectly serious."

It took six months to find a minister who would marry them. A few friends gathered, but neither family would attend.

GO TO PAGE 178 AND LOOK FOR ■2

BRING ON THE FANTASY!

Here's what's happening:

■1 JENNIFER: Having decided that all systems are go and that anything that feels so right has to be right, Jennifer can hardly keep her mind off Jeff. Reading a romantic novel fans the flames, and like the heroine, she pictures herself "limp, languid, and in love" in Jeff's protective arms.

■1 JASON: Jason discovers that Suzy means what she says. She's unwilling to become sexually involved with him. But his overactive fantasy life makes thinking of her in other than a sexual way very difficult. Everybody fantasizes—even Christians. Don't they?

Before we continue with their stories, let's talk about some of the things Jennifer and Jason should know about fantasies.

Bring on the Fantasy!

Everybody fantasizes. Through fantasies we can practice and review actions in a safe setting—our minds. While you listen with rapt attention to what your geometry teacher is saying, your classmates are in worlds of their own.

For example, Tom looks like he's listening, but the only angles he cares about are those he'll ski down on "deadman's drop" and the "screamer" when he hits the slopes after school. Virginia gets the proverbial shivers up her spine as she envisions Tom picking her up for their long-awaited date Friday night. Rachel hardly notices the flurry of activity around her during lunch. In her mind she has been thinking about the speech she has to give fifth period. She imagines herself dropping her notes and the whole class laughing. For the tenth time, Brian rehearses how he'll tell his parents that he has decided not to go to college. At the suggestion of his psychology teacher he imagines himself successfully expressing his points and his parents taking the news well.

But there can be problems with fantasy. Rachel's fantasy only increases her anxiety about giving her speech, and Virginia is setting herself up for a romantic involvement with someone she barely knows.

Fantasies can be harmful when they reinforce fear, nurture emotions for inappropriate partners, or keep us from dealing directly with a problem. The Bible says, "As [a person] thinks within himself, so he is" (Prov. 23:7 NASB). Much of modern psychology is based on that principle. Therapy calls for analyzing, understanding, and changing the way a person views life because thoughts can lead to actions.

Scripture also tells us to renew our mind (Rom. 12:2) if we want to live life in a new way.

Fantasies can set people up for what is to come. A healthy married man or woman thinks lovingly and erotically of the spouse, assuring a joyful and pleasurable time together. A young dating couple anticipate their time spent together by reviewing the traits they enjoy in one another or the fun they will have. But if they are wise, they will stop short of imaginings that result in physical arousal.

Healthy fantasy enriches and nourishes a person's life, but uncontrolled fantasy is the cornerstone of lust and self-defeating behavior. If your fantasies are causing you problems, show them you are in charge by renewing your mind.

1. On a small piece of paper you can carry with you, write out a couple of thoughts or pictures that you find relaxing, fun, or peaceful.
2. When you find yourself slipping into a fantasy that causes you to feel badly about yourself, expect failure, or become aroused physically, react as quickly as possible. Openly or mentally yell STOP, pinch yourself, or snap a rubber band on your wrist.
3. Replace the unhealthy fantasy with one on your list. Do this consistently as quickly as possible *every time*. Consistency will help you develop a new way of thinking. It can eliminate obsessive thoughts of someone or something in about two weeks.
4. Then congratulate yourself on controlling your thoughts and fantasies instead of letting them control you. Congratulations!

What happens next?

■1 JENNIFER (cont. from page 26)

The doorbell announced that Jeff had finally arrived—although, in Jennifer's mind, he had been with her for the last 45 minutes. How could she not think of him? The sight of that athletic build in his tight practice uniform burned itself into her mind. "Hi, Jeff, come on in," she greeted him. "I'll be ready in a minute." She tried not to sound too eager.

"Great news, Jennifer!" Jeff announced with a big grin. "My folks are going to a high-school reunion and won't be back till late. We have the house to ourselves."

Jenny quickly tried to translate what that might mean. An extra spray of Charlie perfume as she ran out the door seemed to calm her butterflies. *Don't give it another thought,* she told herself. *We've always stopped in time before. Tonight's no different.*

The drive to Jeff's house was filled with excited chatter about his college interviews, cheerleading practice, and the upcoming rivals in the next game. Soon they had a fire roaring in the fireplace and a pan overflowing with popcorn between them. "Take that," shouted Jeff as a strategically aimed kernel bounced off her nose.

"You beast!" Jennifer shouted, returning the favor. The Popcorn War raged on, and within minutes the popcorn had commandeered every nook and cranny. Surveying the ravages of war, they fell laughing into each other's arms.

"Oh, Jeff, I think of you all the time."

"I love you Jennifer. I love the way you smell, the way you look."

Kisses replaced conversation as desire replaced reason and bare skin replaced clothes.

"Maybe we should cool off," Jennifer murmured halfheartedly.

"But I love you, Jennifer."

Caught up in the passion of the moment, they couldn't stop their petting short of intercourse. They hadn't planned for this to happen.

GO TO PAGE 31 AND LOOK FOR ■1

■1 JASON (cont. from page 26)

Suzy's hand was on the door. "Jason, if you don't stop this, I'm not going to ride with you anymore."

"But, Suzy, a guy's different. We don't just turn off the hormones because we go to church. Have a heart." Jason put on his best pitiful look, but he could tell it wasn't working.

"Being a guy or a gal doesn't have anything to do with being able to turn off a turn-on."

Jason clinched the steering wheel with both hands. "Well, tell me the secret, will you? I just don't know how," he said in exasperation.

"Why don't you talk to our youth pastor?" Suzy suggested. "He's single. He ought to be able to help. I'm telling you, Jason. I really like you, but this is not a game with me. I have no intention of having sex before I'm married."

"I'm not asking for intercourse," Jason defended. "I just like to touch you. It's normal to want to be close if you like someone."

"You're right. It's normal, but its not always the best. God wants the best for each of us. And we can't play games, pretending we're 'holy' just because the penis hasn't gone in the vagina if we've done everything else. He knows our heart."

Jason was surprised at Suzy's conviction and openness. He had never heard a girl talk so frankly before. As he thought about it, he realized that hardly anyone he knew talked seriously about sex. Most people only joked about it.

Suzy continued, "I don't get involved in petting, Jason, because I know myself. I'm afraid I would like the feelings it produces and it wouldn't take much for me to pass a point of no return." She smiled that great smile of hers and reached over to touch his arm. "You see, you and I aren't so different after all. We're just at different locations on the same road."

He took her hand and kissed her fingers. "I think I'll make an appointment to talk to the pastor."

GO TO PAGE 198 AND LOOK FOR ■1

CHOOSING WHEN TO HAVE CHILDREN

Here's what's happening:

1 JENNIFER: Jennifer's hormones had overridden her brain. The fantasy of falling into Jeff's arms did not include any unromantic activities like opening a condom, making sure it fit correctly, or removing it as soon as ejaculation occurred to prevent the escape of semen. Such interruptions would definitely put a damper on the mood, as would a diagnosis of pregnancy or disease. Jennifer had two loves: Jeff and a romantic notion that a person could have sex with no preparation and no consequences. (After all, on television 40,000 acts of intercourse are depicted annually, and no one ever becomes pregnant or contracts a disease.)

Before we continue with Jennifer's story, let's look at some hard facts about birth control.

Choosing When to Have Children

Bartholomew wanted a divorce. He had been married two years, and still there was no child. Like other Hebrew men in Jesus' day, producing a son was his legacy and indicated his partnership with God in creating life. But last week that new teacher, Jesus, appeared on the scene and for the first time Bartholomew had doubts. This man Jesus did not accept such reasons for divorce. His teaching on the permanence of marriage suggested there were other reasons for being married besides having children.

Bartholomew had read about "two becoming one." Proverbs taught him to "delight in the wife of his youth," and Song of Solomon spoke of the romantic delight a man and woman were to find in sharing their bodies with one another. Could it be that the sexual relationship was also to be revered because of its ability to provide pleasure?

Today few would dispute Bartholomew's revelation. Sex in marriage was designed for more than having babies. Improvements in birth control have enabled couples to emphasize the pleasure of sex to such an extent that little thought is given to other facets. Although we applaud the spontaneity now allowed, we must mourn the loss of having to count the cost and of determining our priorities.

Birth control has been in existence for many generations. Camel dung was once considered effective. Sheep intestines provided the first condom, and undoubtedly there were a few rituals and incantations as well. Only recently, however, have devices been developed that are safe, reliable, and varied enough to accommodate the sexual habits, personal convictions, or particular time of life of the individual.

Eighty percent of sexually active teenagers, five million of them, fail to use birth control. The only teens who consistently use contraception are those who are very active or are in stable relationships. Readily available birth control information doesn't determine whether or not a teen becomes sexually active.

Why don't teens use birth control? It isn't because they don't know about it. But many teens, through no fault of their own, lack the maturity to relate today's actions to future consequences. They don't believe pregnancy can happen to them. So they are willing to take chances.

Many other teens don't do any advance planning because they won't admit that they are sexually active. Girls, especially, prefer to think that it "just happened," because it sounds more romantic. This line of thinking doesn't make much sense if they would realize that they are created sexual creatures, capable of powerful physical desires which they can control.

Other teenagers set out to become pregnant or get someone pregnant. Pregnancy is seen as a resolution to all kinds of personal problems. Instead, they make the situation worse. Teens who make such choices often have poor home lives or lack a good father-child relationship. Girls seek love, touch, and approval from someone else as a substitute. Boys strive for manhood—but their concept of manhood, and how you achieve it, is warped.

NATURAL METHODS. The oldest method of contraception (any method used by one or both partners to prevent pregnancy) world wide, is *withdrawal* . In this practice, the man withdraws his penis from the vagina just before ejaculation, releasing the semen outside the vagina. As a result of misjudgments in timing and of sperm being in the "pre-ejaculate" fluid, perhaps a more apt name would be Russian Roulette.

The *rhythm method* of birth control requires that couples abstain from intercourse during the time that ovulation (the release of the egg from the woman's ovary) is most likely to occur. The trick is figuring out when that is. Today there are some products on the market and a few procedures a woman can perform that help pinpoint that time more precisely. But none of these methods is foolproof.

THE PILL. Unquestionably, the pill is the most widely used method of birth control. It is considered low risk for women under 35 who have normal blood pressure and cholesterol and are not obese, diabetic, or smokers. It has no long-term effect on future cycles or fertility. If taken as directed, it is highly effective in preventing pregnancies.

BARRIER METHODS. The use of barrier methods of birth control has increased in recent years because of their convenience. They are often preferred by women who do not want a permanent type of birth control yet wish to reduce their risk of acquiring a sexually transmitted disease. Many of the barrier methods are treated with spermicide.

The *condom* (rubber) is a widely used barrier method which, if properly used, helps prevent pregnancy and disease. Condoms are inexpensive and readily available and are most effective if treated with spermicide.

A *diaphragm* is a soft rubber cap placed in the vagina to cover the cervix. It, too, is most effective when used with a spermicide jelly, creating a physical and chemical barrier. Diaphragms must be fitted by a physician and rechecked for size periodically, especially after pregnancy or significant change in weight.

A variation of the diaphragm is the *contraceptive sponge.* It is effective for 24 hours, but must be kept in place (like the diaphragm) for six hours after intercourse. The ease of purchase is offset by possible side effects such as toxic-shock syndrome, allergic reaction, and difficulty with removal.

Spermicidal agents are most effective when used in combination with other methods of birth control. Available as creams, jellies, suppositories, and foams, they are inserted immediately before intercourse.

Although all of these methods are more effective than the ones traditionally tried by teenagers (Coca-cola douches, Saran Wrap condoms, standing up for intercourse, staying partially clothed, or not having an orgasm), none is 100% effective and all have some disadvantages. There is currently no male contraceptive other than the condom that most users would label satisfactory.

The most common type of birth control for couples who have been married at least ten years is sterilization. It should always be considered permanent even though in a few cases it can be reversed. Both men and women can undergo surgery that prevents either the sperm or the egg from reaching a place where fertilization could take place. However, the surgery for men (vasectomy) is a far simpler procedure than that for women (tubal ligation).

Both partners must agree upon birth control decisions before engaging in intercourse. A healthy sexual relationship should not be based solely on reduced risk of pregnancy and disease, but there are some questions that need to be answered honestly:

1. Can you talk openly about taking responsibility for birth control and disease control?
2. Will you be able to handle the necessary health procedures if you develop a sexually transmitted disease?
3. Since no birth control is 100% effective, are you ready to raise a child, possibly on your own?
4. Even if you are using birth control to reduce the odds of the most obvious repercussions of sex, are you able to face squarely your motives for engaging in intercourse apart from marriage? Will you be able to handle the feelings that will result from intercourse, such as guilt?

What happens next?

■1 JENNIFER (cont. from page 31)

"How's it going, Jennifer?" Doreen asked as she met her best friend after school.

"Hey, Doreen, let's go get a hamburger. My treat," Jennifer offered.

"Wow! You mean it? You're going to spend time with lil' ole me? What's wrong? Jeff tied up with the team?"

Jennifer flinched at the truth. She rarely had time for Doreen or anyone else these days. She and Jeff had become inseparable. "OK," she replied, "I'll add a sundae to my offer."

At McDonald's, having gotten their food, Jennifer was relieved to see the corner table by the window empty. They could talk there without their conversation making its way around the school crowd quicker than a fax machine.

After getting settled, Doreen bit into her burger hungrily. "What's wrong, Jennifer?" she asked point blank. "You haven't had a minute free for months. Something gone wrong in paradise?"

Tears welled up in Jennifer's eyes. "Lay off, Doreen. I've missed you. It's just that Jeff wants us to spend every available minute we can together. He doesn't seem to want anyone else around."

"I've noticed," Doreen replied with obvious disgust.

"Actually, we aren't getting along too well."

"No kidding! You want a fry?"

"No thanks. I have a feeling it's just about over with Jeff and me, Doreen. I missed my period last month, and things haven't been the same since."

"What? Are you crazy or something? I thought you were planning to go to college!" For the first time Jennifer could remember, Doreen lost interest in her food.

"I know, I know. It's not like we planned on it," Jennifer protested. 'Somehow an opportunity to be alone just happens, and the feelings are so strong we can't resist. We never use birth control."

Doreen shook her head slowly, shifting her attention to her fast-melting sundae. "Dumb, dumb, dumb," she mumbled.

Tears rolled down Jennifer's face. "I don't understand it. Everything was so good at first. Now sometimes I hate Jeff. And as for going on to school, I don't think I could make it in college anyway." She wiped her eyes with a tissue and stared down at the uneaten hamburger before her. "And I've treated my friends so badly. . . They probably could care less whether we're friends anymore or not. I don't have anybody left. At least when Jeff gets ticked, he can still hang around with the guys on the team."

"I'm still your friend, Jennifer," Doreen assured her, "on one condition."

"What's that?"

"That before we walk out of here and go to my place to listen to a great new tape I have, you get rid of the raccoon look."

"Darn mascara," Jennifer said with a hint of a smile. "I guess that's what I get for buying the cheap stuff that isn't waterproof."

IF YOU WANT TO EXPLORE OTHER CHOICES JENNIFER COULD HAVE MADE, RETURN TO PAGE 12 OR 22.

WHERE ARE
THE LINES?

Here's what's happening:

■2 JENNIFER: Jennifer's youth leader pointed out that feelings—even feelings of real love—are not the criteria that determine whether a person should engage in sex. Jennifer understands that, but she needs help in learning what behavior is appropriate for two people attracted to one another.

So before we continue with Jennifer's story, let's come up with some ways to help Jennifer set her own standards of behavior.

Where Are the Lines?

Charles was a chronic rule breaker. He even broke rules that, if honored, would have given him what he wanted! A rule did for Charles what a waving red cape does to a bull. He would attack, batter, and trample on sight. His life motto was: Rules are made to be broken.

Although everyone occasionally strains against a rule, most would prefer (yet never admit it) to have life nicely defined through some list labeled "How to Make Sure Your Life Turns Out Best." Just follow one-two-three and you have it made.

Unfortunately, life is not that easy. It is not always black or white. A simple list of dos and don'ts ignores the many aspects of life that fall into a gray zone. Much of sexual behavior is a gray zone. A nice set of "thou-shalt-nots" for sex would simplify living enormously. But other than the universal biblical commands to *abstain from fornication* (sex between two unmarried persons) and to *flee immorality*, Scripture seems to say little.

That never stops some people, however. Those who like their rules spelled out, gladly fill in between the lines. At one extreme we find: No touching anytime, anyplace, anywhere. Or maybe no touching above the elbows and knees, only outdoors, and only in October. At the other extreme we find those who justify anything as long as the penis is not inserted in the vagina. God wants what is best for his people. He knows the consequences of living life outside of his design. The problem is, we don't see with the same eyes. Our limited vision tells us that right now is all that counts, and anything that feels right must be right.

When rules are not spelled out, doing the wise thing must be the guideline. The wise thing is dependent on an individual's past experience, weaknesses, and strengths. It is more individualized than a general truth meant for everyone. Loosely paraphrased, Ephesians 5:15–17 defines wise living this way: The wise anticipate trouble, make every moment count, and face the facts.

Knowing what is appropriate sexual behavior for the wise person involves first of all admitting that getting involved sexually in the wrong way is a real possibility no matter how pious one happens to be or how convinced that "it could never happen to me." Involvement seldom occurs as the result of one unfortunate big YES. It is commonly the culmination of a whole series of little yeses, most of them innocent and harmless on their own.

Anticipating trouble enables a wise person to develop a plan. Under what circumstances do I want to be sexual? What will the person be like? What will it mean to us? In what physical setting would I like to be when I give the most intimate part of myself, emotionally and physically, to another? Not having a plan makes it

38

easy to go along with the flow, "choosing" to become involved by not choosing *not* to.

Aspirations and dreams are tossed aside or modified when people find themselves somewhere they never intended to be. Time is wasted and may never be recovered. This is why the warning: time is short and we must make every moment count.

Finally, the wise person faces the truth, for truth is wisdom. What does God want for me? Am I open to his plan? How vulnerable am I to sexual arousal? Am I at risk when I date someone who doesn't share the values and faith I have? What are my strengths and what are my weaknesses? This is facing the facts.

Judging whether or not to become involved based on, "if it feels good do it," is not much of a contest. It *will* feel good. God made it that way. Sex is a beautiful, pleasurable, and joyful experience. The situation makes it wrong, not the act.

So where do we set the lines? Having made us the creative individuals we are, the Lord knew that "the line"—the wise way to express our sexuality—could not be spelled out in one generic list. Those well-meaning leaders who try to supply one are endlessly frustrated by people's natural tendency to "line-shop." If this line begins to cramp my style, I'll simply find an authority whose line is more to my liking.

The wise person develops an honest plan for sexual behavior based on God's ideal, learning to control the body in a way that is honoring to him (1 Thess. 4:2—8).

What happens next?

■2 JENNIFER (cont. from page 37)

On a beautiful summer day Jennifer and Jeff finished their stint at the church car wash, walked over to the park, and relaxed in the shade of a big oak tree.

Jennifer propped herself on her elbows and followed the path of two bright yellow butterflies doing their version of a mating dance. "Jeff, are you sorry we haven't had sex?" she asked.

Jeff sat up quickly. "Why would you ask that?"

"I heard some girls talking in the cafeteria the other day, and they said that sex is what makes a relationship for a guy."

Jeff seemed uncomfortable. He didn't look directly at her for a few silent moments; then he said, "I sure think about it a lot. I think you're beautiful, Jennifer—I really do. I wonder what it would feel like. But all of that stuff Bill has been talking about in youth group—"

"You mean about God having a best, number-one plan for us?"

"Yeah. That made sense to me." He seemed more at ease now. "I would like to make love to you, but I also like being your friend, and talking to you, and learning all about your plans and dreams. For me, there is more to you—and to us—than your body, as attractive as that is!"

Jennifer rolled over, shifting her attention to the clouds. "The part that made the most sense to me was when he helped us figure out the things we were doing that made staying away from sex so hard—like being in your house alone or always dating alone."

"Or watching some of those videos!" Jeff let out a howl that sounded like a heartsick wolf. Jennifer laughed.

"It's really been easier since then, hasn't it?"

"Who would have figured it!" he said. He hopped up and starting to run. "Last one to the pond pays for lunch!"

GO TO PAGE 41 AND LOOK FOR ■2

OPPOSITES ATTRACT

Here's what's happening:

■2 JENNIFER: This falling in love stuff was a lot more complicated than Jennifer first imagined. Sure, there were romance and feelings of attraction, but deciding if someone was right for you—for life—was no snap decision. Discovering shared dreams and values was also part of the puzzle of falling in love and getting married.

We'll continue Jennifer's story in a minute; first, let's help her learn to evaluate her long-term compatibility with her boyfriend.

Opposites Attract

Remember the last time you had to do a team project at school? You were assigned to Joe Cool, the fellow who comes when he feels like it and then only to catch up on his sleep. The beautiful report that bore both your names was a product of *your* last-minute blood, sweat, and tears. You had long since given up on any contributions from him. Working with someone whose value system, view of life, and work habits are just the opposite of yours is the pits!

But when it comes to relationships, many adolescents choose to get involved with boyfriends or girlfriends whose basic life view is just as different as yours and Joe Cool's. Young people often ignore the biblical command: "Do not be yoked together with unbelievers. For what do righteousness and wickedness have in common? Or what fellowship can light have with darkness?" (2 Cor. 6:14). They do not ask the probing questions. They give only superficial attention to differences. "After all, we don't intend to marry," they say. But the truth is, we aren't likely to marry someone we don't date!

Even when Christians don't marry the non-Christians they've been dating, they spend a lot of time with someone who can do nothing to bring them into a more consistent walk with the Lord. And they often find themselves in settings where they are even less likely to meet others that share their values.

It is amusing to watch two mutually attracted people search out what they have in common. Each is thrilled to discover that the other adores old Beatles records, hates soccer, and loves pizza. Obviously, they were meant for each other! They don't, however, know how the other feels about marriage, having children, who should do the housework, going to church, and what to spend money on. Delving too deeply may prove they aren't as alike as they wish to be, so they avoid some of the most important issues. To discover what a person is really like, your dates need to include an opportunity for talk and serious probing to see beyond personality, looks, and popularity.

Realistic appraisal of who you are can save considerable heartache in choosing your companions. God never asks us to make things look better or worse than they are. How much do you really have in common with your dates? Do the kind of people you go out with help you maintain your ideals and standards? Think about the unhappy marriages you know about. What issues tore at the foundation of that marriage which probably began with the greatest expectations?

What happens next?

■2 JENNIFER (cont. from page 41)

"How do you do it?" Maxine asked. "Three children of your own, a never-ending stream of foster children, and you and Jeff act more like newlyweds than newlyweds." It wasn't a rhetorical question. Maxine sincerely wanted to understand. She was not the only person who sensed a difference in Jeff and Jennifer's marriage.

Jennifer poured a second cup of coffee for each of them and plopped down on the couch. "Sometimes it gets pretty hectic around here." Pushing back a twist of hair that refused to stay in place, she shot up a silent word of thanks to God. He had given her and Jeff the strength to choose His best plan for their lives. "For one thing," she continued, "Jeff and I spent many hours together talking and sharing before we married."

Her friend wrinkled her nose. "Weren't you afraid you'd discover things that you would disagree on and blow the whole romance?"

Jennifer couldn't help but smile. "Of course we didn't agree on everything, but we made sure we agreed on the important issues like lifestyle, children, and faith before committing to marriage."

"Still sounds risky to me." Maxine helped herself to another cookie.

"It was. But any pain it might have caused at that stage of the relationship would never equal the pain of ending a marriage," Jennifer said honestly. "I knew, for example, that Jeff didn't care about having a large and fancy house. Right from the start he told me he preferred to take major family trips once a year and live more moderately."

"And you agreed with him?"

"I had to give it plenty of thought, but I decided I could live with that. Of course, an extra bathroom would be nice!"

Both women laughed.

"What really helped, though, is that we entered marriage without hangups—physical or emotional—over previous sexual relationships. We came to the marriage pure, and our wedding night

43

was really symbolic of the commitment of giving ourselves only to one another."

"That's so romantic," Maxine said. "Frank and I lived together before we married, so on our wedding night he went to bed early to rest up for a 6:00 AM golf game!" Her misty eyes and nervous giggle revealed her pain.

IF YOU WANT TO EXPLORE MORE OF JENNIFER'S CHOICES, GO TO PAGE 12 OR 22.

MASTURBATION: VICE OR VIRTUE?

Here's what's happening:

✱✱ JENNIFER: When Jennifer was a little girl she discovered she could produce pleasant feelings by rubbing her genitals. She's never heard any of her friends admit they've made the same discovery, so sometimes she feels a little guilty about doing something no one talks about. She wishes she knew whether it is right or wrong but doesn't know anyone she could ask. Sometimes she decides to "play it safe" and never indulge again. But then the urge becomes overwhelming, and she gives in "this one more time." Is it wrong? Is she the only one?

Let's continue Jennifer's story as soon as we try to answer some of her questions.

Masturbation: Vice or Virtue?

When I taught a human sexuality class at a local community college, I would ask my students to write an essay, tracing the development of their sexual value system. One paper I have never forgotten was from a young man in his thirties. I'll call him Scott. His story clearly points out how something healthy and normal can be made into an unhealthy preoccupation—all in the name of morality.

Scott's mom noticed fluid on Scott's pajamas, and she was livid. Instantly she forced him to dress, then drove him to church where he had to confess his "sin" to the priest. Imagine his humiliation and confusion! The fluid was the result of the normal, healthy process of night emission, the release of seminal fluid that builds up when there is no regular release through intercourse or masturbation. It is common in young teenage boys.

The experience was so traumatic that making sure it never happened again became an obsession—and, so did masturbation. Scott eliminated the possibility of accidental emissions by establishing a pattern of masturbating five or six times a day. His mother had reinforced the exact behavior she feared.

Some people seem to get hysterical about a behavior that is not even mentioned by name in the Bible. Some mistakenly cite the story of Onan (Genesis 38) as proof of God's disapproval of the practice. In truth, however, Onan was a greedy man who failed to impregnate his dead brother's childless widow as was his duty under the Hebrew law. Instead, at the last minute, he "spilled his seed upon the ground," that is, he withdrew his penis and ejaculated outside the vagina. That practice was an early form of birth control, and it is still practiced by some today though it is not very reliable. For his disobedience to the Hebrew law, Onan was killed.

Early church fathers, seeing the sexual immorality all around them, had trouble viewing sex as a gift from God. Since people were so vulnerable to sexual sin, physical desire seemed an untamed enemy. Surely God intended strict limits on its expression. Woman was a "seed bed," they reasoned, and man planted the seed. This was true in nature, so it seemed natural for human beings, too. They discouraged any further expression, including enjoying the act while fulfilling your duty!

Today, most biblical scholars believe that sex is good in itself, and that God designed it to be a pleasurable gift. For many people, though, old attitudes and reservations persist.

As the church lost its influence over people's lives, social and behavioral scientists took up the cause, making connections between masturbation and poor mental health, poor eyesight, and criminal behavior. Because we now know that such claims aren't true, most opposition to masturbation is based on its being a self-centered practice that has potential for bypassing God's plan for the sexuality of his people.

The time some people spend in personal agony and grief over the practice is clearly out of proportion, since the Bible says nothing directly about it. Why don't they show the same concern over other practices which are specifically condemned, like greed, envy, or overeating? Christians would do well to remember not to speak authoritatively where God has not spoken.

Does that mean that people should masturbate whenever they want and not give it a second thought? No. It means that when the Bible is silent, each individual must do what is wise for him or her. Masturbation is wrong for you if you believe that Scripture forbids it. It is wrong if it prevents you from dealing with personal problems or if you substitute it for establishing a relationship. It is wrong if you are married and use it as a weapon or a means of avoiding sexual intimacy with your spouse.

Some people object to the practice of masturbation because it is frequently accompanied by fantasy. It doesn't have to be. A person can focus on the physical sensations. For a married person, thinking of the spouse is legitimate, but for the unmarried person, thinking of that cute redhead in science class is lust. The single person can offer praise to the Lord for the partner God will provide someday and for the joy of a healthy, responsive body.

Though some would argue that focusing on physical sensations is a selfish use of something intended to be shared, we all indulge in many solitary pleasures. We use our voices (which were given to us to communicate) to sing in the shower. We immerse ourselves in the beauty of a sunset. We are creatures made for relationships, but we can be renewed and refreshed by times of solitude.

For some with high sexual drives that cannot be met by a spouse, or whose spouse is ill, away, or has less sexual drive, masturbation is definitely a preferable alternative to adultery or fornication, which is strictly forbidden in the Bible.

Masturbation can relieve tension, give assurance that bodies work in a healthy and normal way, or simply provide pleasure. Those who imagine God as harsh and judgmental find it hard to believe that the Lord wants us to experience sexual pleasure (even though he provided an organ on the female, the clitoris, with no other purpose). Whatever you personally decide is God's will for you, do not, by your judgment, be a stumbling block to the faith of a Christian brother or sister (Rom. 14).

The Apostle Paul says that everything is permissible but not everything is good (1 Cor. 10:23). So we need to look at our heart motivation:

1. Am I "addicted" to masturbating?
2. Is it a new god?
3. Does it hinder building a healthy relationship with the opposite sex?
4. Is it the loving thing to do?
5. Have I been led to better emotional health and a greater sense of well-being, or has it led to increased worry and guilt?

What happens next?

** JENNIFER (cont. from page 45)
Jennifer uses masturbation in response to her feelings of arousal. She can choose to direct her thoughts toward the physical sensations of her body and her thankfulness for the relief and pleasure God has provided her. Or, she may focus on Jeff and their physical relationship. Is this a solution that is right for everyone? How will Jennifer do in handling her thoughts and desires?

**1. Jennifer keeps her sexual arousal under control through occasional masturbation. She doesn't find it necessary to

fantasize about Jeff.
GO TO PAGE 50 AND LOOK FOR **1

**2. While masturbating to get relief for her sexual tension, Jennifer inevitably fantasizes about Jeff.
GO TO PAGE 62 AND LOOK FOR **2

THOSE POWERFUL URGES

Here's what's happening:

**1 JENNIFER: Sexual feelings and thoughts are not beyond our power to control. Jennifer's ability to feel sexual pleasure is made possible by the way God designed her body. In fact, her clitoris was apparently included in the design for no other reason than to experience pleasure. And the urge to experience sexual pleasure, and to spend time thinking about it, is very strong—but not uncontrollable.

Let's see if we can understand more about the powerful urges Jennifer experiences—and then we'll continue her story.

Those Powerful Urges

You probably have a favorite restaurant. Its atmosphere suits you, and you are rarely disappointed with the food. Just the thought of returning puts you in a good mood. On the other hand you may dread returning to a restaurant your friends adore because you can't forget how ill you became after eating there. You may remind yourself that it was simply a coincidence, but logic doesn't change your reaction.

Sometimes what is found a turn-on or a turn-off sexually is also the result of a random event. Those who, as infants, were handled unkindly or discouraged from touching their bodies in any way that might bring pleasure, probably will not believe that their bodies should be a source of pleasure. Pleasurable or unpleasant experiences of the past (whether remembered or not) can cause men to become preoccupied with women's legs or breasts and can cause women to be turned on or off by a man's bulging muscles.

Most people become aware of sex appeal at a very young age. By adolescence the interest intensifies and certain combinations of qualities lead them to be attracted to one person over another. Chemicals released in the brain give a sense of pleasure and certain physical reactions announce, "I find this person attractive." The body's first quick response to what the person finds erotic is not a conscious choice.

Sometimes teenagers find themselves in situations they never intended to be in because no one ever told them how powerful erotic urges can be. And no one ever told them that these urges feel good. So, frequently they assume that the relationship they are involved in must be right "because it feels so right." No one has told them that sexual arousal feels good because God made sex to be pleasurable. Off-limits people and settings can often be the most attractive. If we're not aware of this, we can be both fooled and foolish.

This is why parents and pastors often warn young people about their dating habits. A couple who spend many hours alone together frequently battle powerful impulses that escalate until control appears impossible. But, given the right setting, anyone can unexpectedly become overwhelmed by feelings for someone he or she would not normally be attracted to. Not having planned on anything like this, the person becomes confused and doesn't know what to do, so he or she just "goes along." Powerful urges to become more and more intimate are even more difficult to control if your will power has been altered by drugs or alcohol.

Sexual arousal builds powerfully and quickly; soon, it seems that a sexual act *must* follow—but that really isn't true. Your arousal cools off quickly when a policeman shines a light into a parked car, and passion vaporizes when Mom and Dad come home an hour early. But choosing to cool down a body that has been responding to the type of foreplay God designed to end with intercourse, breaks a normal, pleasurable escalation of events, and it is difficult.

Some people have a hard time controlling their sexual appetite, just like some people eat too much. Others find living a sexual life that glorifies the Lord simple. Pious attitudes, condemnation, or denial of our individuality solves nothing. Each person must accept responsibility for living sanely, wisely, and compassionately as God's sexual man or woman. That is why God has not spelled out a universal list of dos and don'ts for righteous relationships.

When the "thou-shalt-not" lines aren't spelled out, we are to live wisely (Eph. 5:15). You need to know your body well enough so that you can maintain control (1 Thess. 4:3–4). And after you decide what lines are wise for you, you should also consider the vulnerability of the person you care about. No one is to take advantage of anyone sexually (1 Thess. 4:6). Controlling powerful urges is not easy, and we have to wonder why God didn't provide a less complex system. But we *can* control our sexual urges. To think or act like we have no control is to deny the strengths God gave us when he made us.

What happens next?

**1 Jennifer (cont. from page 50)

"Jeff, I have to tell you something." Jennifer's shiver was not due to the cool night air as they walked along the river bank.

"Uh-oh! This sounds bad." Jeff frowned. "Your great aunt is sick and you have to move to Alaska?"

"No, silly." Jennifer laughed, but her mood quickly became serious again. "This is hard for me to share, Jeff, but—I really, really like you."

"Is there a but?" Jeff asked uneasily. "There must be a but."

"Yes—I'm worried that my feelings for you are too strong," she explained. "When I'm around you I feel—pardon me—

horny." There, she said it. He probably would never speak to her again. Why couldn't she have just kept her big mouth shut?

Jeff smiled the sweetest smile and looked deep into her eyes. "I know that feeling, Jennifer. It must be communicable."

Her heart did a flip-flop.

"Jen, I don't want to have sex with you. I mean I do," he hurried on, "but I don't intend to. I believe that intercourse is for marriage."

"Oh, Jeff, I thought you would think I was awful for bringing it up. I was afraid I'd have to break up with you if I couldn't get my feelings under control."

"Whoa, that's not necessary," Jeff assured her. "Since we both want the same thing, I'm sure we can come up with something." He slipped his arm around her, and she snuggled closer. They picked up their pace. "When is it worse for you?" he asked.

"It's always harder for me when we go out on a date with just the two of us. You open the car door for me, and it's like someone opened the floodgates to my hormones."

He laughed and she gave him a playful punch. "I think it would help if we did more group dating," she said.

"I agree. Sounds better than those icy showers I have to take when I've dropped you off after a date. But I know something else we can do."

"What's that, include my kid brother?"

"Nothing that drastic! I think we ought to confide in Bill down at the church. If someone is holding you accountable, it's harder to mess up."

"Good idea! He's single and he's talked about people he's accountable to. Let's talk to him Thursday night after youth group."

Jennifer felt as though a huge weight had been taken off her shoulders. And she felt even closer to Jeff.

GO TO PAGE 54 AND LOOK FOR **1

A PERSONAL PLAN
FOR SEX

Here's what's happening:

**1 JENNIFER: Good intentions, they say, are a dime a dozen. Jennifer's acceptance of herself as a responsive, sensuous design of God is healthy. Her decision not to deny or give in to her desires is noble. Lots of people make that decision. Many don't follow through. To stick to it she needs to develop a plan.

■2 JASON: Jason and Suzy's relationship continues to grow, as does Jason's faith. He really can't imagine that he will be able to control his sexual feelings. He never has! It helps to understand that there is a reason for control. It isn't just "ruining his fun." He wants God's best. He and Suzy spend several hours talking through a personal plan for their sexuality for each of them. Jason feels encouraged. It just might work.

**1 MICHELLE: The defenses were in position. Now that Michelle had changed her behavior, worked on her forgiveness, and become accountable to a small group of friends, it was time to look forward and establish the offense. She knew what she *didn't* want to happen; now the focus needed to shift to what she *did* want. She had to adopt a personal plan.

Before we continue with Jennifer's, Jason's, and Michelle's stories, let's talk about how to develop a personal plan for sexual behavior.

A Personal Plan for Sex

One of the most common questions people ask writers is, "How do you actually write a book?"

The answer many writers give is, "Decide what you want to do, develop a plan, and stick to it." Lots of people have wonderful stories running around in their heads that don't get written because they never get past the great-idea stage. Self-discipline and a clear plan transform dreams into reality.

In a study done at Yale University, business graduates were asked about their monetary plans for the future. Only five percent of the class had clear long- and short-range plans to meet their specific goals. After twenty years, those five percent made more money than the other 95 percent combined! Knowing exactly what they wanted to do helped them establish a plan to meet their goals.

Personal goals are not just for writers and businessmen. Take Brian, for example. His dad bought him a used pickup on his sixteenth birthday. It needed some fixing up, but Brian was thrilled. He worked hard over the summer, earning money to make the minor repairs and purchase the necessary accessories, parts, and paint that would make it a showpiece.

After a year, to Brian's disappointment, his truck was anything but a showpiece. All the paraphernalia he had added looked like someone had dropped a shopping cart on it. The police informed him that the oversized tires and additional height would have to go, and an annoying glitch he had never spent enough time to find, left him stalled at red lights. Though hilarious to his friends, it was embarrassing to him.

Brian's problem had nothing to do with money. He had spent plenty on his dream. But things had not turned out well because Brian had forgotten to develop a plan, an overall approach which spelled out his priorities. If he had, unexpected windfalls and hard-earned cash could have been used to complete the next priority rather than to go in some dead-end direction that more than once had to be undone. Plans help people focus on their priorities. Brian learned a hard lesson about the necessity of planning before undertaking a project he valued.

High school juniors and seniors pore over college bulletins to ensure that the college they pick is right for them. People pay thousands of dollars for tests and analyses to assure that their job will meet their needs. Yet few give much thought to a plan for sexuality. They approach sex haphazardly, and like Brian's truck, it doesn't turn out as expected.

A plan increases the odds that your desires will be fulfilled. Every teenager needs to spend time planning how to express and use the gift of sex.

Is it just for recreation or restricted to use within the bounds of a marriage commitment? Is it important that sex be pleasurable in marriage? Do you want to experience a sexual relationship without guilt and free from disease? Ultimately, what do you want sex to mean to you? How specifically can you make your goals a reality?

Under what circumstances will sex occur for the first time? Where will you be? Will it be after a wedding that has announced to everyone that you have made a permanent commitment? How about a romantic honeymoon following an intimate family service in the same church in which your mom and dad were married? Will your partner be a romantic stranger you'll never see again? Will your partner be a serious but not-interested-in-marriage type or someone who is capable of a lifetime commitment? Will your first experience take place in the back seat of a car? in a motel? a honeymoon suite? hurriedly at a friend's home? How will you spend the next day? What will you both be doing before you share the most intimate aspect of life two people can share? How will you feel about yourselves afterwards? What will you be wearing? Will there be music? flowers? a warm bath?

Having a clear plan for your sexual life helps you evaluate the situation you are in and determine quickly if this is the way it is supposed to be. You can't make this kind of clear-headed analysis or develop a plan when your body is sending messages for ever-more-intimate behavior! But if you already have a well-defined plan, you know when your behavior is getting out of sync with that plan. Any deviation can flash a red light in your mind as passion-cooling as the unexpected slamming of Mom and Dad's car door outside. When you realize that the setting is wrong, your emotions quit racing, and you have a second chance to take responsibility for living your sexual life the way that promises best.

What have you done about developing your personal plan for your sexual life? What goals do you have? If you haven't done any planning, "your book idea is still just rolling around in your head." Do you really want to risk that it will never be written?

Get out a piece of paper. Decide what you want to happen with your sexual life. Plan how you want your story to become reality. Stick to it!

What happens next?

**1 JENNIFER (cont. from page 54)

Jennifer gathered up the remains of a midnight feast. "Doreen, want another slice of pizza before I put it away?" she asked, balancing the box precariously in one hand and scooping up glasses with the other.

"Naw," her friend replied, "I figure if I lose five more pounds, Randy might notice more about me than the fact that I get A's in biology."

"Oh, stop it," Jennifer chided. "If he doesn't love all of you, he's not worth it!" The pizza box landed in the garbage with a thud for emphasis.

"Speaking of love, how goes it with the dynamic duo?"

"You know, it's funny, but ever since we talked about our fears that our feelings might get out of control, we've been closer than ever. It's been great having time to do our own things, too."

Doreen began her own version of aerobics, lying across the bed. "Gee, I would have thought that would make you less close," she said.

Jennifer tried to keep a straight face as her friend managed two of each move, including those real killers—the finger exercises.

Inspired, Jennifer began doing situps. "No, we always have stuff to talk about," she said.

"Do you think you'll marry Jeff?"

Jennifer stopped her situps to ponder Doreen's question. "I dunno. I know we really love each other—maybe."

IF YOU WANT TO EXPLORE JENNIFER'S OTHER CHOICES, GO TO PAGE 12 OR 48.

2 JASON (cont. from page 54)

Jason's dad slammed the door so hard that it shook the house. The two of them had been working on the car when Jason told his dad that he had become a Christian.

His dad started yelling and chased Jason inside. "You wimp!" he screamed. "I knew you'd changed since you started hanging around with that girl!"

Jason flinched but didn't say anything. He turned toward the sink and gazed out the window.

"Next thing you know she'll have you quitting the team so you'll have more time to read the Bible," his dad growled. He shook his head in disgust. "All I can say is she must be great in bed!"

That's the last straw! Jason thought. How could he honor a father who behaved like that? Jason swung around, ready for anything.

His father tensed, obviously sensing they had crossed some invisible line.

Jason clenched his teeth and stormed out of the room. Banging into a chair, he knocked down one of his mother's favorite plates. It crashed to the floor just as his mom entered the room.

She opened her mouth to speak but Jason's father yelled at her—"Leave him alone!"

Ignoring her husband's protest, Jason's mother entered his room a few seconds after Jason flung himself onto his bed, sobbing. Closing the door gently behind her, she sat on the edge of the bed and placed her hand on his back.

It had been years since Jason had cried, and the tears flowed like a dam had broken. *Oh, why can't things be like they used to be B.C.—before Christ,* he thought. *Maybe Dad was right. Maybe it's not worth it.*

When the tears quit coming, he turned and faced his mother. "Mom, I don't know what to do," he admitted. "I didn't want any part of this Christian stuff, but somehow I just couldn't ignore it."

His mother handed him a tissue and he blew his nose. "What is it that is special to you, Jason?" she asked.

"I guess the most important part for me is that Jesus took all the punishment for my sin so that I can live with him forever."

"That sounds like a mighty loving God to me."

Jason sat straight up, grateful but surprised that his mother seemed to understand. "He loved me enough to die for me, but you know, Mom," he said, "Dad doesn't even love me enough to listen to what is important to me, let alone die for me."

"Nobody on earth is perfect, Jason," Mom replied. 'I guess we have to love one another anyway, shortcomings and all."

Jason was seeing his mother in a new light. Had she always been so wise? Like his dad, Jason loved her but saw her mainly as "chief cook and bottle washer." That was the way Dad always introduced her.

"Mom, I want you to know I'm not having sex with Suzy," Jason told her. "I can hardly believe it, actually—but you know that; I've talked to you about this before. I've always gotten turned on so easily, and I usually don't even try to stop. But even though we're not doing any of that stuff, I'm closer to Suzy than I've been to any other girl."

Mom didn't even blink. "Sounds to me like you have a good thing going, Jason," she said, "all the way around. Come on, let's see how good we are at gluing plates back together."

IF YOU WANT TO EXPLORE OTHER CHOICES JASON COULD HAVE MADE, GO TO PAGE 14 OR 104.

1 MICHELLE (cont. from page 54)
Several years later. . .

Dr. Greenberg's office was not coldly professional. Pictures of his family adorned the walls, and the soft lighting made it seem more like a living room than an office. Today, however, Michelle did not feel at home. Dr. Greenberg's nurse had asked her to come in and get her test results from the doctor in person. That was not a good sign.

"Good morning, Michelle," the doctor's voice shattered the silence. Wasting no time, he took a seat at his desk and turned to face her. "We've been through a lot together, haven't we?"

She nodded but said nothing. The memory of her tubal pregnancy, the frantic rush to the hospital, the bleeding, were all still fresh in her mind even though Rebecca was born one and a half years later.

Dr. Greenberg continued, "Your pelvic inflammatory disease has thrown up lots of roadblocks—the tubal pregnancy, infections, infertility—but you have been blessed. Rebecca is a beautiful, healthy baby girl."

Michelle brought out the latest picture of her 18-month-old and handed it to him. They had tried to have a baby for so long. Now Rebecca was the joy of their lives. But who would have guessed that so much heartache could have been caused by her promiscuous behavior as a teen.

"She looks happy and loved," he said as he handed the photo back to her.

"She is," Michelle finally managed to say.

"I'm glad you have her," he said, "because I'm afraid I have some bad news."

Michelle braced herself.

"Your test indicates that you have cervical cancer," he said softly. "You'll need a hysterectomy. I'm sorry, but there is no mistake and no way to delay it while you have another child." He leaned over and placed his hand on hers.

Tears began to roll down Michelle's cheeks. "Doctor, is this related to my earlier behavior too?" She looked straight at him, knowing she could depend on her gynecologist to be honest with her.

"Probably so," he admitted. "The chance of cervical cancer goes up radically with the number of partners you have been exposed to. And from what you've told me, you were rather active sexually."

"But I changed!" Michelle protested. "It seems so unfair. I've been a faithful wife. And I know the Lord has forgiven me. All that was so long ago!" She hesitated, straightened in her chair and asked slowly, "He has forgiven me, hasn't he?"

"Don't doubt that for a minute, Michelle. Never confuse the consequences of sin with lack of forgiveness."

Mistakes from the past continued to haunt Michelle. A hysterectomy spared her life, but of course she couldn't have any more children. If she had known, would it have made a difference? Would she have changed her behavior? Would you?

IF YOU WANT TO EXPLORE OTHER CHOICES MICHELLE COULD HAVE MADE, GO TO PAGE 16 OR 83.

I "LUST" YOU

Here's what's happening:

**2 JENNIFER: When Jennifer is on a date with Jeff, remembering the pleasure and romance of her fantasies turns her on even more. She can hardly keep her hands off him. At home her mind focuses more and more on their physical relationship. Jennifer clearly has a problem with lust. Lust has a one-track mind, focusing on a singular dimension: our selfish desire for the other person. Lusting does not bring out the best in either the "luster" or the "lustee."

** JASON: Jason "loves" the way Cathy's tight skirts tend to mold around her bottom when she wiggles by. She appears to be every guy's living fantasy. There is no question she enjoys the "I'm undressing you" looks. Jason's not "in love." He's "in lust."

We'll continue Jennifer's and Jason's stories as soon as we've talked about how lust might affect them.

I "Lust" You

What *is* lust? Is it that first bodily response to something arousing? No. That immediate and unsolicited reaction is not under your conscious control. Once aware of your bodily reactions, however, you can choose to nurture or extinguish them. Lust begins when you decide to pursue the response. In other words, Charlie Brown is not lusting when he is enamored with the little red-headed girl—unless he lets himself imagine her undressing for him.

Lust reduces that little red-headed girl to a sex object. The fact that she is a talented musician, is compassionate, a good cook, and a whiz at science no longer matters. So Charlie's relationship with her is limited.

A lot of people joke about their sexual thoughts, but Jesus didn't take the thought life lightly. When asked about it (Matt. 5:28), he said that looking at someone and imagining yourself sexually involved is as serious as actually doing it.

He set such a high standard that it's futile for us to try to live a righteous life on our own! Fortunately, God offers Christians supernatural power and guidance. The Holy Spirit helps us do what would be impossible alone.

Essentially, lust is a silent sin. Your forehead doesn't break out with satanic horns, but those who wrestle with it say that its drivenness, distraction, and guilt rob them of their peace of mind.

Besides praying and asking for the Holy Spirit's help, those who lack peace can direct their thoughts to "whatever is true, whatever is noble, whatever is right, whatever is pure, whatever is lovely, whatever is admirable. . ." (Phil. 4:8). That verse and the next makes a promise: "If anything is excellent or praiseworthy—think about such things. Whatever you have learned [from Scripture]—put it into practice. And the God of peace will be with you."

If you have gotten into the habit of mentally undressing every attractive person of the opposite sex you meet, you can put this passage into action by quickly substituting another preplanned thought to replace the usual lustful one. It is like switching tapes on a tape recorder. A new tape may not erase the memory of the old one, but substituted regularly, it can effectively change your thought life.

When Charlie Brown's thoughts for the little red-headed girl go beyond admiration of her as a total person, he may wisely substitute the thought of a romp in the park with Snoopy or playing football with the gang. Or he may prefer to quote Scripture to himself: "I can do everything [even break lustful habits] through him [God] who gives me strength" (Phil. 4:13).

What happens next?

2 JENNIFER (cont. from page 62)

Jennifer was glad no one else was home as she and Gloria sat talking over a pizza in Gloria's kitchen. She had to confide in someone, and her friend listened eagerly.

"Wow!" Gloria exclaimed. "I don't know what to say. I mean, it sounds like you and Jeff are having a hard time keeping control."

"That's the truth," Jennifer answered. "Hand me another Pepsi, would you?" She tried to sound casual, but her head felt like it was on fire. "I've tried just not thinking about it. I've tried keeping our dates in public places—very public places." She opened the Pepsi noisily and took a drink.

"Like shopping malls?"

"Exactly," Jennifer replied. "And we still end up breathing heavy in his car when we kiss goodnight. But even worse, after he goes home, I go right to bed and think of all the things we could have done." She gobbled down a big bite of pizza. "And then I think the same kind of thoughts when I look up in algebra and see him smiling at me." She wiped the pizza sauce from her hands.

Gloria sighed deeply. "Well, true confession time," she said. "You've got the same problem with Tim?"

"Not really. But I used to with Charlie," Gloria admitted.

"Ah."

"Yeah. So I learned some techniques for dealing with it. Want to hear?"

Jennifer nodded eagerly and Gloria told her about "thought-stopping," renewing the mind and focusing on thoughts that bring peace and distract you from unhealthy thoughts. It took most of a pizza and a six-pack of Pepsi before Gloria and Jennifer decided that the most pleasant thoughts Jennifer could substitute for lustful thoughts of Jeff were images of a sunny day of skiing or memories of her special sixteenth birthday party.

"Hey," Gloria giggled as they finished off the pizza. "I've got an idea. It'll be great fun."

"Order another pizza?"

"Ooh, yuck. I can't eat another bite. No—what about inviting Kelly and Doreen over for Friday night? I happen to know that both of them are having a hard time saying no to their boyfriends—or to what Kelly and Doreen would like to do with their boyfriends. We can talk this same thing over with them, and we can all think up ways to tell boys 'no' without sounding like we're prudes or like we really don't like them."

"Sounds great," Jennifer said.

And so they did.

GO TO PAGE 67 AND LOOK FOR **2

** JASON (cont. from page 62)
Jason does not understand that fantasies lead to action. Cathy enjoys the impact she makes—especially with Jason. It makes her feel womanly and desirable. Neither realizes that they are playing with matches which, when struck, will blaze with trouble. Or, are we overreacting? Maybe fantasies are just harmless imaginings, like the world says. Make a choice for Jason:

**1. Jason seizes the opportunity to score. He makes a date with Cathy when he knows her folks are out of town. Fired up by his thoughts of her, he doesn't intend to take no for an answer.
GO TO PAGE 116 AND LOOK FOR **1

*⸸*2. Jason and Cathy look for as many opportunities as possible to be together; nothing else really matters to either of them any more except their relationship. The more intimate they become, the more they want—and dream about. Soon they're having frequent sexual relations—but without the benefit of birth control.

GO TO PAGE 120 AND LOOK FOR *⸸*2

RENEWING THE MIND

Here's what's happening:

**2 JENNIFER: Jennifer is pleased to have some techniques to help refocus her thoughts. Spending nearly every hour of the day craving Jeff's body does not make her happy or productive. Thought-stopping is a helpful tool for getting "unhooked" from obsessive or distracting habits.

We'll continue Jennifer's story as soon as we find out why "thought-stopping" might work for her.

Renewing the Mind

Perhaps you've had days when you wished you could trade in your mind for a new model. Maybe you've experienced what a guy named Mac did. He thought he was going insane. He had just broken up with Julie, but he couldn't keep his mind off her. He was glad they had called it quits. Both knew they should have broken up months before. And yet, every place Mac looked he saw Julie's face or thought of something they had shared. Depressed and worried, he wondered whether he would *ever* get her off his mind!

Mac was a Christian and was familiar with the passage in the Bible that talked about the type of change that can happen by "renewing your mind" (Rom. 12:2). He knew he needed "a new mind" but wasn't at all sure how to go about it. Brain surgery was obviously out. He had prayed and consciously tried to think of other things, but he still needed help.

Mac had a friend who was a Christian counselor. He asked her for advice, and she told him about a technique that helped people who felt trapped by obsessive thoughts. She asked Mac to develop a list of pleasant events or places that did not involve Julie or experiences they had had together. He listed them on a 3 x 5 card and placed them in his shirt pocket. Then when a thought came that he was trying to replace, he didn't have to waste time deciding what to think about. He simply took out the card.

His friend suggested that the procedure would be even more effective if the moment he became aware of an unwanted thought, Mac yelled STOP, popped a rubber band on his wrist, or pinched himself. He was to keep track of the number of times he had to use the technique and commit to using it consistently.

Mac found that thought-stopping helped him feel he was in control. As his friend had warned, in the first week there were days when his thoughts of Julie actually increased, but with consistent use, by the end of the second week Julie rarely crossed his mind.

Doing this consistently for at least two weeks takes time and effort. But you waste more time and effort if you remain preoccupied with a former love. And you may need to practice the procedure a few times before you can do it "for real." But a renewed mind is worth the effort.

What happens next?

**2 JENNIFER (cont. from page 67)

Jennifer hung up the phone and walked into the kitchen to find out what that wonderful aroma was. "Hi, Mom," she said, smiling. "What's for dinner?"

"Was that Jeff on the phone?" Mom asked. "You two seem to

be getting along exceptionally well these days. And we're having pot roast, by the way."

"M-m-m, the kind with the tomato sauce, I hope."

Mom took the pot roast out of the oven and lifted it onto a hot platter. "You're in luck," she replied. "But what's happened between the two of you?"

"Prying, Mom?" Jennifer asked with a mischievous grin.

"Just interested in the romantic attachments of my little girl," Mom said, a little too defensively.

"Well, actually Mom, it's a bit personal, but since you're such a busybody—" Stalling, she ran her finger through the mashed potatoes and masterfully manipulated a hunk to her mouth.

Her mother looked horrified. "Jennifer! Stop that and get on with your story."

"Well, Jeff and I are finding it easier and easier to 'cool it' on our dates, Mom," she explained. "A couple of our friends are holding us accountable, and we're being careful about our day-dreams. It's neat to be able to talk about it openly between us. We can even joke about it, and we're always finding something new and different to do." Jennifer finished her story by snitching a little piece of pot roast.

"Jennifer, if you don't quit helping yourself, there won't be anything left to put on the table," Mom scolded playfully. Then she gave her daughter a quick hug. "I'm glad you've been able to work things out, though," she said. "It says a lot about your character when you have the self-discipline to look beyond the moment." Stopping her dinner preparations, she looked straight into Jennifer's eyes. "I'm proud of you, honey. I can see that you both truly care for one another."

For the first time, Jennifer felt a little embarrassed, "We do care, Mom, but we're taking one day at a time and making sure we don't do anything to jeopardize our future." She put her arms around her mom. "Say, why don't I take the food in to the dining room while there is still something to take?"

"Good thinking," Mom said with a smile.

IF YOU WANT TO EXPLORE OTHER CHOICES
JENNIFER COULD HAVE MADE, RETURN TO PAGE
12 OR 48.

TEEN SEXUAL RELATIONSHIPS

Here's what's happening:

○ JENNIFER: Jennifer knows girls from school who mysteriously dropped out because, according to rumor, they were pregnant. Usually it didn't surprise her. But, Jennifer reasoned, she and Jeff are different. They are *really* in love. Nothing like that could happen to them. Or could it?

Jennifer is about to make a life-changing decision. Let's talk about it, and then we'll continue Jennifer's story.

Teen Sexual Relationships

Most teen movies imply that there aren't any virgins over the age of fifteen. The truth is, close to half of all graduating high-school seniors have *not* had sexual intercourse. And most of those who have wouldn't begin their sexual life with the same partner if they could start over.

Sometimes the motivation to begin having sex is simply to get it over with and see what all the fuss is about. Increased spare time, often unsupervised since many mothers are at work, provides opportunities that were less common in the past.

Every sexual relationship, no matter how casual, affects a person's sense of self, interpretation of sexuality, and general health. So if you don't want to tangle with the complications of what you are doing, don't have sex. Abstaining is a lot safer emotionally, physically, and spiritually.

According to research, girls tend to feel that they have found everlasting love, and they expect to marry their sexual partner. But teens rarely fall in love forever. Often the first "love" is the beginning of a series of relationships.

Frequently, boys mistakenly believe that sexual intercourse proves them manly. So, when the two agendas inevitably collide, someone, perhaps both, will suffer.

Since the media portrays a person's first sexual experience as spontaneous, many teens don't even think about planning it. Yet this is an event that can occur only once in a lifetime. Unlike the media version, a person's first sexual experience is almost always awkward, messy, and disappointing. Rarely are young partners able to convey what they really need and want, an essential ingredient in enjoyable sex.

Just letting sex happen is not romantic or spontaneous. It is stupid. Most young people do not use birth control the first time. Such "free love" proves to be far from free. Despite improved medicines, more and more people suffer long-term damage, including chronic illness, sterility, tubal pregnancies, miscarriages, stillbirths, birth defects, and STDs (sexually transmitted diseases). A girl who is sexually active before seventeen may double the risk of developing severe cervical dysplasia (precancer) or invasive cancer. Besides the physical scars, teen sexual activity often results in broken relationships, forced marriages or separations, upset or broken homes, abortions, and illegitimate babies.

A teen love affair which thrives on "being alone together" stifles social growth at just the time it should be expanding. And it can sabotage future sexual adjustment. Sexual intimacy is powerful stuff!

The costs of early sexual relationships far outweigh any physical pleasures or shortcuts to emotional closeness. In any other area of a healthy young person's life the risks would be considered too great compared to the rewards. But today's society doesn't encourage clear thinking when it comes to sex. Hormones don't have brains! Ask yourself the following questions:

1. If you are involved with someone sexually, does your sexual relationship have the same meaning for both of you?
2. How would you feel if you had a child and could not raise it in a stable, two-parent home?
3. Have you thought about the number of people who could potentially be affected by your "private" decision to have a sexual relationship?

What happens next?

○ JENNIFER (cont. from page 71)
Jennifer had dreamed that a satisfying sex life would seal her and Jeff's love. But somehow sex seemed more like a horror show than a great romantic epic. Maybe their experience was not so different from other teens' after all. Jennifer is disillusioned with sex and with Jeff. How will she handle it?

○1. Constantly worrying about getting pregnant, Jennifer longs for the way things used to be, when her only major medical concern was a pimple. She decides to break up with Jeff.
GO TO PAGE 74 AND LOOK FOR ○1

○2. Jennifer feels uncomfortable with the sexual relationship she and Jeff share, but since she has gone so far, she feels she can't go back.
GO TO PAGE 84 AND LOOK FOR ○2

HOW TO FALL OUT
OF LOVE

Here's what's happening:

O1 JENNIFER: Jennifer finds that, like the song says, "breaking up *is* hard to do." She wants out, but everywhere she goes she is reminded of Jeff or something they did together, and she gets depressed. She longs to get him off her mind and "fall out of love."

We'll look at some ways she can do that, and then we'll continue her story.

How to Fall Out of Love

Deciding to end a relationship is often easier than doing it. No matter how sure you are that you want to break up, memories of things you loved about the person and sometimes things you didn't care for, persistently haunt you. Maybe you love someone who doesn't love you, and getting that person out of your mind is a trick you can't seem to master.

Begin the healing process by asking God to free you from the memories of the person you love. Claim the promise that "we are no longer prisoners of sin" but free in Christ. Then, do *your* part. Conscientiously follow a plan that will help you think of the person less often and reduce the intensity of your feelings.

Make a list of the most positive scenes or sayings (including scripture) that you can think of. Make sure none of them has anything to do with the person you've been preoccupied with. The Bible calls this "renewing your mind."

Because we tend to idealize people we love and still have to be around them after a break-up, we may need to use another technique. Sometimes we need to change the way we see that person. Imagining the former love-of-your-life in an absurd or comic situation often helps. (But don't visualize scenes that are vindictive or evoke sympathy for them!)

For example, Thomas was infatuated with Brenda. He spent most of his time thinking of her. But when she made it clear that she was not interested in pursuing a relationship with him, Thomas had a hard time "falling out of love." She was in two of his classes and was a cheerleader at his games. Since Brenda was fastidious about her appearance, Thomas imagined her cheering at a game with her hair in curlers, picking her nose. Such an absurd picture quickly eliminated the heart-in-the-throat feelings that had nearly incapacitated him before when she was near.

Barbara had such a bad crush on her English teacher that she couldn't concentrate in class. She melted at even the sight of his smile. But she was able to put her feelings in perspective when she imagined him smiling with no teeth!

Nurturing your own healthy self-concept can also help you survive a love that can no longer be. For a Christian, self-worth comes from knowing we are adopted children of our heavenly Father. He will never stop loving us. In him we can maintain a healthy sense of belonging and being loved that we'll never find if we depend on the whims of others or substitute things like a job, status, success, money, or cars.

It's easier to change your behavior if you tell a trustworthy friend your desire to be free of distracting or obsessive thoughts and fantasies. If you are afraid to admit your struggles to someone else, that's natural. But remember that Christian fellowship includes upholding one another.

So, how do you fall out of love?

1. Call on God to help you claim your freedom.
2. Reduce the amount of time you think about the person. Whenever the former love comes to mind, substitute positive scenes and thoughts that don't include that person.
3. If necessary, reduce the intensity of your feelings through humor, imagining them in some outrageous way.
4. Do anything that helps you maintain a positive self-concept. For instance: Review the Scriptures that tell you that you're God's Somebody. Or learn something new. Or do something good for someone else! Exercise!
5. Make yourself accountable to a good friend.

What happens next?

O1 JENNIFER (cont. from page 74)

As Jennifer lay on her bed, the loud ring of the phone on her nightstand made her jump. Why couldn't their phone have a little chime like the Simpsons' did? It seems so much more civilized. "Hello," she said in a slightly groggy voice. Apparently she had dozed off studying Mr. Connel's World War I notes. Mary's bright voice brought her fully awake.

"Oh, hi, Mary. . . . No, you didn't interrupt a thing except World War I, and I had already put a hold on it! . . . How am I doing? Well, I want you to know that I have reduced the number of times I think of Jeff from a high of fifty times a day to three or four times. . . . Thanks. I think it's great, too. Hey, y'know what else? I started working as a volunteer at the hospital. I really like the kids in pediatrics. . . . Yeah, yeah, you were right. Things are getting better. A lot of the credit goes to you and your encouragement. . . . Well, you can say it's not much if you want, but I couldn't have done it without you. I knew that breaking up with Jeff was the *right* thing to do. I just didn't know it would be so *hard*. Are we still on for tomorrow night? It's the anniversary of when Jeff and I met. I need to do something fun. . . . Great! I'll see you then."

Putting down the phone, Jennifer thanked God for her friend Mary. It was nice to have someone you could depend on to help you through rough times!

GO TO PAGE 78 AND LOOK FOR ○1

HOW TO SAY NO

Here's what's happening:

O1 JENNIFER: Jennifer feels that life is on the upswing—but she doesn't want to find herself back in the same situation again. Learning to say no to further sexual involvement has actually proven to be fun as well as effective. The following list is just a start. Talk to your friends and add your own ideas to the list.

** MICHELLE: It is never fun to be hit in the face with unpleasant truths about yourself. But the more important issue is what we decide to do about it. Michelle has the option of saying no in future encounters.

Saying no to sexual advances isn't always easy, but both Jennifer and Michelle need to learn to do it. Let's talk about it, and then we'll continue their stories.

How to Say No

Remember your first driving lesson? How about your first school dance? Pretty awful, right? Doing something you have never done before feels awkward. You feel self-conscious. After a few run-throughs, however, you become a pro and can handle yourself with ease.

Saying no to sex is sometimes easy—when it's someone really obnoxious, for instance, or someone you just don't find attractive and don't feel threatened by. But it can also be the worst kind of awful to say no to someone you're afraid of, or who you really *really* like, or who you want to impress. But you *can* do it, with practice. You might want to have some lively conversations with the mirror, but you could also try devoting a youth group program or overnight with friends to practicing the fine art of saying no.

What are you going to do if someone says, "I'll leave you if you don't have sex with me?" or "What's wrong? Are you a prude or something?" or "You've been coming on to me for days. What are you, a tease?"

First, you have a perfect right to say no. Nowhere is it written that a person must have sex because someone says they should. There are lots of legitimate reasons for not having sex, including: religious reasons, being scared, knowing it is not the wise thing to do, and simply not being ready.

Yet according to one study, 43% of 15- to 18-year-old boys, 65% of 15- to 16-year-old girls, and 48% of 17- to 18-year-old girls report having been pressured for sexual contact when they didn't want it.

You may recognize some of the "come-ons" listed below.[1] You and your friends can add to the list of replies.

Come-ons	Comebacks
1. *The Lover:* "If you really loved me, you'd do it." "I just want to show you how much I love you."	"If you really loved me, you wouldn't pressure me." "That isn't the only way we could express our love."
2. *The Rationalizer:* "Everybody's doing it." "You know you really	"If everybody is doing it, you won't have any trouble finding someone else! And

Come-ons	Comebacks
want it, too, so why not?"	anyway, I'm not everybody." "There are some things I want more."
3. *The Educator:* "It will show what it feels like to be a man/woman." "You won't know what it feels like until you try it."	"I'm protecting my future. I don't intend to play adult games." "I'm not going to do it just so I can see what it's like. I want to be ready and really love the person."
4. *The Flatterer:* "You really turn me on—you're so beautiful/handsome."	"I'm glad you find me attractive, but wouldn't you like to get to know something about me besides the physical?"
5. *The Guilt-Tripper:* "You owe it to me." "You're a tease."	"No, I don't. I owe myself a lot more." "I'm real close to my dad, and he has sworn that if anyone ever tries to get me to do something I don't feel good about, he'll take care of him. You aren't trying to make me do something I don't want to do, are you?"
6. *The Name-caller:* "What's wrong with you, anyway?" "You don't want to be a prude [or a drag], do you?" "Are you inhibited or something?"	"What's wrong with *you*, anyway? Don't you know what no means?" "Actually, I'd rather be a prude [a drag] than sorry." "I'm not inhibited—I'm cautious. I guess my self-worth is more important to me than taking the risks you're asking me to take."

Come-ons	Comebacks
7. *The Manipulator:* "If you don't do it, I'll leave you." "If you don't do it, I'll tell everyone you did, anyway." "It hurts to love you so much and yet hold back. I feel so frustrated."	"So long." "If we *do* it, *I'll* leave *you.*" "Losing someone who threatens me would be more gain than loss." "Pardon me. I need to call home." "Love is worth some sacrifices."
8. *The Activist* (the one who's all over you): "Come on, it's just part of the game."	"Dating you is like being out with an octopus." "You seem to be into the physical. Read my lips: N–O!" "I have to go home. I think I left something on the stove." "No, no, no." "Take me home." "I think you need a shower to cool off."

Practice builds confidence and enables you to get out of awkward situations. Humorous responses are especially helpful because they break the tension and allow the mood to change. Most importantly, sharing the problem with friends who have similar values provides a system of accountability. This is one of the most practical ways to ensure that your behavior stays in line with the standards and values you hold.

Although there seems to be a "conspiracy of silence" about sex, you can break it. Be brave and talk openly with someone you trust. If you don't feel comfortable discussing your sexual struggles with your parents (even though your parents also heard the same lines!), confide in a youth leader or a good friend. You may be surprised at how much support they can give you.

Think through your philosophy of sex. Know what you believe and why. Pray regularly about your sexual life.

Relax. Even when your friends aren't around and passion has made all those clever sayings evaporate, one Special Friend is still with you—even in the back seat of a car, on your couch at home, or in the great outdoors. He promises, "No temptation has seized you except what is common to man. And God is faithful; he will not let you be tempted beyond what you can bear. But when you are tempted, he will also provide a way out so that you can stand up under it" (1 Cor. 10:13). Now that's a friend you can rely on!

What happens next?

O1 JENNIFER (cont. from page 78)

Several years later. . .

"Oh, Darren," Jennifer sighed as they hurried across the university campus, "do you realize that we graduate in 25 days and our wedding is only 31 days away?"

Darren smiled. "I never thought I would find anyone as special as you, Jennifer," he said.

She loved his openness and his forgiving spirit. When their relationship began to get serious, she had mustered all her courage and confessed her high school relationship with Jeff. She was sure he would call the whole thing off. Instead, he just asked her if she had asked God for forgiveness and if she had forgiven herself.

Jennifer took his hand. "I'm so glad we believe in a God who is able to make broken people whole again," she said. "Thanks for insisting that I talk to Pastor Tom. Ever since I accepted the fact that I'm a new person in Christ, I've been able to feel good about being with you instead of thinking of myself as 'tarnished goods.'"

Suddenly Darren stopped, pulled her over to a nearby bench, and looked lovingly into her eyes.

Jennifer felt her throat get tight.

"Jennifer, I forgave you when you told me about Jeff," he said tenderly. "But I'm also glad that your reputation here at school is so good. Before I ever went out with you, I heard about this bright, beautiful girl who was able to keep a guy in line in a way that made

82

him like her even more. You learned from an early mistake and made a previous weakness a strength. I like that."

Tears welled up in Jennifer's eyes. She had never loved Darren more than she did at that moment. "Thank you," she said softly.

"Come on," he said, "I don't think Professor Figgins will be nearly so forgiving if we're late for class."

IF YOU WANT TO EXPLORE JENNIFER'S OTHER CHOICES, GO TO PAGE 12 OR 73.

✲✲ MICHELLE (cont. from page 78)
Michelle has a dilemma. She has made a mistake and needs to consider some changes. This could be a real test of character. Will she overcome a "sleazy" reputation, or will she seek vengeance on those who used her? What will she choose?

✲✲1. Michelle learns to say no to promiscuous sex and finds that she no longer feels used. This helps her self-image somewhat, but her past behavior still makes her feel guilty and unworthy.
GO TO PAGE 216 AND LOOK FOR ✲✲1

✲✲2. Michelle is angry at the willingness of guys to use her, cast her aside, and then make fun of her. For a moment she considers never letting them have their way with her again. She decides instead to make them pay. She'll extract her vengeance by seducing them on her terms.
GO TO PAGE 191 AND LOOK FOR ✲✲2

THE CHOICE OF ABSTINENCE

Here's what's happening:

○2 JENNIFER: Jennifer has discovered that sex is not the take-it-or-leave-it proposition suggested by the media. Sharing your body has meaning beyond the act itself. Consequences go beyond the physical. She wishes she could roll back the clock, but choosing not to be sexual once you've crossed that line seems futile, silly, and much too hard. Does Jennifer have the option of abstinence, or is it too late?

○2 MICHELLE: Michelle had come to the right place. After several weeks of counseling, she accepted the Lord's forgiveness for her sin and rededicated her life to him. For a while she drifted from one dull, routine job to another. But eventually, she decided to return to school and took a job at a day-care center to support herself. Even though Michelle wasn't sure what the Lord had in store for her, she chose to live sexually pure, remained open to his will, and felt her life had a sense of purpose.

○2 ERIC: When Eric began to associate with other homosexuals, he found that many of them doubted their orientation could be changed. Some, like Eric, had sought counseling, prayed earnestly, and used willpower to be "cured." When that did not happen, many decided to live with "the hand the Lord (or Fate) dealt them." Often, that meant they chose to actively participate in sex with same-sex partners. Those who take this route ignore God's design that all singles abstain from sexual relations—whatever the reason.

Michelle, Eric, and Jennifer face a difficult choice: Should they abstain from all sexual relations—is it even possible? Let's continue their stories as soon as we've considered their options.

The Choice of Abstinence

Choosing abstinence is choosing not to have intimate sexual relations with anyone. You'll get a lot of pressure if you take such a stand. Some will say that it's a sure sign that you're hung-up about sex. Others will say that if you remain celibate, you'll sacrifice your peace of mind if not your sanity. They'll say abstinence is impossible.

Nobody says it's easy, especially if abstaining from sexual relationships makes you feel deprived. We always want what we cannot have. If we diet, we crave a fudge brownie or ice cream sundae. If we are placed on the alternate team in volleyball, we long to be on the "A" team. Making the choice to be celibate will not work if it feels like deprivation. You need a reason to make the choice, or it makes no sense to say no.

Abstinence makes sense if you choose it because God promises that it's the best plan for your life. Although it's a tough choice, God does not intend it to be some perverse test of holiness. Be assured it does not cause physical or mental harm.

Since God was the one who decided to make men and women sexual, his plan will obviously work best. He tells us that the most fulfilling sex is that found in healthy marriages. If we choose anything less, we subject ourselves to diseases which can affect our future fertility and health; emotional disappointments; relationships in which each partner has a different emotional investment;

lowered self-esteem as we give away cheaply something of great value; and feelings of emptiness and being used. Worst of all, we naturally feel distant from the God whose design we choose to ignore.

It takes a great deal of self-discipline to choose abstinence. You have to focus on more than your own self-centered needs and take charge of your sex life instead of letting it take charge of you. You have to be honest and alert to learn where you're vulnerable.

You'll have a terrific reward on your wedding day, however, when both you and your partner can pledge your love and the gift of pure bodies to one another. The ceremony takes on tremendous symbolism for everyone involved.

"It is God who works in you to will and to act according to his good purpose" (Phil. 2:13). The trick is to trust that God's plan for your life is good. And, what if you fail? "Put your hope in the Lord, for with the Lord is unfailing love and with him is full redemption" (Ps. 130:7).

How do you choose abstinence in a world that says it's impossible?

1. Refuse to let others set your standards for you.
2. Trust that God's plan is ultimately the best for you.
3. Analyze your actions. Are they in the best interest of the other person?
4. Make sure that physical satisfaction is not more important than discovering who you are or what the person you love is really like.
5. Base your involvements on reality, not fantasy.
6. Never use sex as a way of avoiding or resolving other problems.

What happens next?

○2 JENNIFER (cont. from page 84)

As Jennifer careened angrily down the school corridor, she bumped into Joel. "Next time don't take up the whole hall and you won't be hit!" she yelled over her shoulder at him as she hurried on.

"Jennifer!" Doreen's sharp tone stopped her short. "What's wrong with you? Somebody cancel your cable TV or something?"

"I'm sorry." Jennifer meant it. "I'll find Joel at lunch and apologize. I'm just having a bad day."

"Try bad week—or month," Doreen corrected. Her expression revealed her confusion over Jennifer's recent behavior. "If you ever want to talk, Jenn, just give me a call."

Oh, did Jennifer want to talk! But how could she tell anyone what she was battling with? After you've become sexually active, it isn't easy to change your mind and habits. She kept hearing an instant replay of her dad's favorite expression: "You've made your bed, now lie in it." She'd made her bed, all right—literally.

GO TO PAGE 91 AND LOOK FOR ○2

○2 MICHELLE (cont. from page 84)

Michelle delighted in the late afternoon sun that peeked through the trees as she walked up the church steps. She still wasn't sure why she had been asked to attend the meeting of the Board of Elders. But this was a large, active church in a major metropolitan area, and she assumed the meeting had something to do with the children's pageant for the fall.

Tom McPherson, head of the elder board, greeted her at the door. "Come on in, Michelle. We're ready for you," he said warmly. He was a tall, sometimes gruff man, but Michelle had always liked him.

Michelle followed Tom into the meeting room and received warm welcomes from the six other elders present. As she took her seat, for the first time she felt a little nervous. She knew all these men but sensed the formality of the occasion.

Tom sat at the head of the table and picked up a gavel, casually twisting it in his big hands. "Ray, why don't you go ahead and tell Michelle why we've invited her here," he said.

Hmm, thought Michelle, *I guess this isn't about the pageant after all.* She turned and gave her full attention to Ray.

Ray stood up and his voice sounded official as he addressed Michelle and the other elders. "We have been considering establishing a pregnancy counseling center here at the church for quite some time," he explained. "If we are going to take a stand against abortion, we must offer an alternative that will help people get through this difficult time."

He paused and went on. "Michelle, a number of us have followed your growth and your work at the day-care center. We want to establish a place where women who decide not to abort their babies can leave them while they seek help or do what's necessary to get their lives in order."

"Oh, that's a wonderful idea!" Michelle agreed. "It's so needed."

"Well, we'd like more than your moral support," Ray said with a little laugh. "We would like you to run the child care part while our counseling center handles the counseling and information area."

Mr. Smith, an accountant, said, "You would be placed on a salary and be a staff member of the church."

Mrs. Wilkerson sat forward and picked up her coffee cup, "We want you in charge because you have overcome such difficulty in your own life, and your work with children and parents at your present job has prepared you well."

Michelle sat speechless, her mind racing. *Lord, how faithful you are! I thought my time at the day care-center was just a job, but it's been preparation! Thank you!* Regaining her composure, she replied, "I would love to take on that responsibility!"

Tom silently placed the gavel on the table in front of him. "We'll work the details out later," he said. "Today we just wanted to know if you would consider this opportunity."

Michelle did take the job. The pay was somewhat less than she had been making, but she had the bonus of knowing she was where the Lord wanted her. Her responsibilities required flexible hours and unusual requests, but since she was single, she could be there whenever she was needed. Her empathy and dedication to making each child feel wanted made the center a success.

If only such a center had existed when she had faced her own pregnancy.

IF YOU WANT TO EXPLORE OTHER CHOICES MICHELLE COULD HAVE MADE, GO TO PAGE 16 OR 169.

O2 ERIC (cont. from page 84)

Loud voices drifted into the pastor's office from the conference room. Pastor Jim, deciding he had better check on the commotion, stuck his head through the doorway. The voices immediately lowered.

"Hi, guys, what's the problem?" he asked.

"Not a new one, I'm afraid," said Blake, a dark, handsome man in his early thirties.

Jon sat up straight in the overstuffed chair that looked like it could swallow him. "You know, Pastor—the usual stuff. We get tired of sex being off limits to us."

Pete stood by the window, looking a little like he wanted to escape through it. "Let's face it—I'm a young guy and I like sex. How can I go without it?"

Leaning against the wall and taking his time, the pastor finally spoke up. "Nobody said it was easy. But it's no harder for you, Pete, than it is for any other single person or spouse with an ill or absent husband or wife. We were made with the desire to want to be intimate with another."

"But Pastor," Pete protested, "the heterosexual single can look forward to getting married. Or the spouse can get well or return. I'm *not* heterosexual—what have I got to look forward to?'

Eric, who had been listening patiently, went over and put his hand on Pete's shoulder. "You know, Pete, each of us has his own sexual drives to battle, so I'll never be the first to throw stones, but it comes down to trust."

"Trust?" Pete asked.

"Trust," Eric replied. "Trusting that your life will turn out better if you don't act on your sexual desires. Trusting that God's plan is best."

Pete took a chair near the rest of the group. "It's sure not easy," he admitted. "And it doesn't seem fair."

Pastor Jim thrust his hands into his pockets and smiled. "It will help if you quit focusing on what you don't have and put your energy into all the things you do have going for you," he encouraged.

"That really helped me," added Brad. "I *would* like someone to be with—but my life is so full already. I wouldn't be able to do half the things I do if I had a family."

Eric looked directly at Pete. "The Bible tells us to carry each other's burdens," he reminded him. "When yours get too heavy, let us help."

Eric had come a long way. For the moment, God had not chosen to remove his same-sex desires, but each year he found greater strength to live with them in a holy and honorable way. Lately, he had been an encouragement to Pete and others who struggle with strong sexual desires.

IF YOU WANT TO EXPLORE OTHER CHOICES ERIC COULD HAVE MADE, RETURN TO PAGE 18 OR 196.

FEELING CRUMMY ABOUT YOURSELF

Here's what's happening:

○2 JENNIFER: Strange things happen to our minds when we've made a mistake or—let's face it—a dumb choice. Jennifer's feelings about herself are so low, she thinks she deserves what she gets. But she decides she can redeem something of her self-image if she just hangs in there.

**1 JASON: Jason was confused. He thought he knew all about women. He would never force himself on someone who really didn't want it—or at least that's what he thought until last night. Cathy may have asked for it, but he had been pretty rough, and she was genuinely hurt afterwards. His buddies would understand—they'd have done the same thing. "Bagging" women is what makes a man a man, they reasoned. Jason doesn't understand why he feels so low.

You may have felt some of those same feelings yourself—so let's examine those feelings before we continue with Jennifer's and Jason's stories.

Feeling Crummy About Yourself

It doesn't take much for us to decide that we're lower than a stink bug. Some surveys show that we need ten positive strokes to recover from one negative one. You remember the wrong answers you gave on the test rather than the right ones. And if you're used to a perfect report card, you'll never forget the one that had a *B* on it.

The worst thing about feeling crummy about yourself is the downward spiral it often initiates. One thing happens, then another, and pretty soon you are convinced that there is no one else as inept, ugly, zit-filled, and stupid. At this point, some decide to bluff it. They may feel like a nerd but nobody is going to know because they go on a self-aggrandizement campaign. When not presenting themselves as the coolest thing since MTV, they make someone else look bad.

Most people just mope around, wishing for a fairy godmother or the Rapture to transform them into an attractive human specimen. They can't quite muster the energy needed to feel better about themselves.

Feeling crummy is common to those who feel they are "nobody." But here's some good news: GOD + YOU = A SOMEBODY. But as in algebra, the formula won't work if any of the parts are missing.

You often feel like a "nobody" when you try to be a "somebody" by leaving out God or replacing him with something else: athletic prowess, intellect, looks, status, money, cars, what people say or think about us, or anything else we value.

None of these substitutes works. We can depend on our friends as long as they don't fall in love, move away, or get an *A* in biology. Even our parents sometimes fail to give us the reinforcement it takes to feel OK.

God is different. Because he has adopted us as his children (Rom. 8:14-16), we share in his status and glory as kids of the King. Jesus loved us enough to die so that we wouldn't have to live under the guilt of our imperfections and failures. We are free to be

Somebody. And the Holy Spirit lives inside every Christian to correct, reassure, and help in every situation of life (1 Cor. 10:13).

If you want to trade in crummy feelings for Somebody feelings, trust God's Word and continually remind yourself of his promises. Resist the temptation to alter the formula. Being God's Somebody miraculously transforms the way you live, helps you love others without judgment, and brings inner peace that you can't find as a nobody or as the world's idea of a somebody.

1. Are you a Somebody, a somebody, or a nobody?
2. If you depend on anything other than God to be somebody, what will you do about the "nobody" feelings when that substitute lets you down?

What happens next?

O2 JENNIFER (cont. from page 91)

While Jennifer sat in the career center waiting for her appointment with the school counselor, she looked around at the bulletin boards that screamed Opportunity! It was a cruel joke to have to wait in a place that promised an unlimited world when her choices had shrunk to near nothing.

Mrs. Dorris's cheerful voice called Jennifer back from her private musings. "Hi, Jennifer. Come on in."

Relieved to be leaving the land of opportunity, Jennifer silently followed her counselor inside and sat across the desk from her.

"Jennifer, it's time for us to review your college plans," Mrs. Dorris began.

Jennifer let out a long sigh. "Thanks, Mrs. Dorris, but I've changed my mind about college," she said. "I'll be getting married after graduation."

Mrs. Dorris searched Jennifer's face hoping to find some hint of the vivacious girl she had last met with. "I don't know how to respond to that," she said honestly.

Jennifer began to twist in her chair. "I'm very much in love with Jeff," Jennifer explained softly. 'We've made a commitment to one another. I'm sure marriage will be an exciting *opportunity*."

"I hope it will be," Mrs. Dorris responded apologetically. "I didn't mean to suggest that I wasn't happy that you have found someone to love. It's just that I see so many kids selling themselves short and not getting further education because they are anxious to take on the demands, responsibilities, and, yes, the rewards of married life. But if that is your decision—" she stood and looked sadly at Jennifer, "—I wish you luck."

Mrs. Dorris's attitude left Jennifer in a bad mood for the rest of the day. No one seemed to understand. Jennifer was convinced that people thought she was unattractive, incapable, and selling out. In truth, Jennifer, herself, felt that way.

GO TO PAGE 96 AND LOOK FOR ○2

**1 JASON (cont. from page 91)

After football practice, Jason trudged into the locker room, his eyes on the floor. It had been a terrible practice. He had dropped three routine passes in a row. His heart wasn't in it today, and his mind was definitely on something else.

Bert looked up from undressing. "Hi, stud. How's it going?" he called. "Don't forget, good buddy. We meet at the principal's office at three o'clock tomorrow afternoon for the inquiry. If we stick together, we'll be partying by four!"

Cindy Norris had accused Bert of date rape, but Bert was getting all his friends to swear that Cindy gave away free what Bert was accused of taking.

Jason had always liked Cindy. She seemed like a nice girl, and she certainly hadn't been sleeping around. As far as he could tell, she hadn't even flirted with any of the guys.

"Are you sure you need me, Bert? Sounds like you have it under control.'

Bert struck a noble pose. "United we stand. Divided we fall," he said dramatically. Then he laughed. "Hey, you score with Cathy yet? When you're ready to move on, let me know. I'll show her what a real love machine is like!" Throwing a towel around his waist, he headed for the showers.

Jason sat dejectedly on the bench. He didn't want to go to the inquiry and lie. He didn't want to see Cathy again, either. He didn't know what he wanted.

IF YOU WANT TO KNOW MORE ABOUT JASON'S OTHER CHOICES, GO TO PAGE 14 OR 65.

WHAT DO YOU DO
WITH GUILT?

Here's what's happening:

○2 JENNIFER: Hampered by low self-esteem, Jennifer is choosing to stay in a situation she has grown increasingly uncomfortable with. Because she is looking at life through dirty windows, she can't see things clearly. She lowers her goals and soon feels she can't take on any challenging tasks. Will Jennifer be able to come to terms with her guilt? Can she make an early marriage an opportunity?

■1 ERIC: Eric has many things working against him. He hasn't been able to check out his questions about being gay with anyone except people who would somehow benefit by his joining their ranks. If he had, he would have learned that everyone develops at his or her own pace and that each person's sexual drive is different. Sex drive isn't a good gauge of sexual orientation. Like most kids, he had experienced some same-sex sexual play and because he enjoyed it, he saw this as more evidence of being gay. Most convincing, however, was his "crush" on his male gym teacher, his dreams, and his fantasies. Now that he has had a sexual relationship, he feels that his fate is sealed. Is this true? Does one sexual experience with the same sex make a person a homosexual? What does? Eric was overwhelmed with guilt and fear.

Let's talk about this powerful thing called guilt, and then we'll continue with Jennifer's and Eric's stories.

What Do You Do with Guilt?

Modern psychology tells us not to feel guilty because we draw on walls, steal purses, or dump on our friends. We cannot help ourselves, it says, because our mothers (it's always the mother) whipped us with wet noodles, didn't read us bedtime stories, or took a job outside the home.

Scripture teaches that guilt is a legitimate part of life. When we choose to do something wrong, we experience guilt. Besides learning about right and wrong from the world around us, each person also has an inner moral sensitivity to good and evil. Guilt waves a red flag that something in our behavior is out of whack.

If you want to overcome guilt feelings, try this: Instead of blaming others, find forgiveness by taking responsibility (see Hebrews 8:10, 12). Jesus has already paid for all your sins: big or small, frequent or occasional, long term or first time. When you can humbly admit that you have sinned and are helpless to consistently live otherwise, God cancels the debt.

Unloading your burden of guilt on Jesus' waiting shoulders is easy. Not taking it back is the tricky part. Feeling forgiven may be instantaneous or involve gradual acceptance. King David acknowledged and confessed his transgressions and asked to be washed clean, but Psalm 32:5 indicates that he also accepted God's forgiveness.

John 8:1-11 tells of an adulterous woman who was brought before Jesus. Caught in the very act, she doesn't have the slightest defense according to Mosaic law. The penalty is death by stoning! But what does Jesus do? He asks those without sin to cast the first stone. Her accusers leave. Jesus himself refuses to condemn her and tells her to go and sin no more.

According to Luke 7, Jesus let a prostitute wash his feet. The men around him were horrified, for this was the age when merely being touched by a woman might render you unclean. A touch by a prostitute must have required a purification offering of five sheep, three oxen, two turtledoves, and a partridge in a pear tree! But Scripture teaches that the prostitute was forgiven because of the faith and love she expressed, not because of her good works (vv. 36–50).

After you have messed up (whether it seems big or small), accepted your guilt, and decided to live God's way, remember the promise in Romans 8:28: "And we know that in all things God works for the good of those who love him, who have been called according to his purpose." Beautiful things spring up from the ashes of life. Only God can make a life new again.

Reread Scripture to remind yourself of his promises. Confide in good Christian friends. Their acceptance and forgiveness make God's forgiveness even more real. Don't focus on your sin and guilt anymore. Accepting God's forgiveness means focusing on him and everything that is pure, true, and good.

When guilt is gone, you have the freedom to risk being all you can be. You can have a close relationship with God because there is nothing to hide. But most importantly, you can like and accept yourself because you are a redeemed person.

What happens next?

O2 JENNIFER (cont. from page 96)

A couple of years later. . .

"Stay out late if you want to!" Jennifer yelled after Jeff. "I don't care if you ever come back!" Her last threat was drowned out as Jeff slammed the door, leaving for a night out with "the guys."

This argument had to be number 364 for the week. And the previous week they simply hadn't talked to each other. She couldn't decide which made her more miserable. Her heart sank as she turned to face a sinkload of dishes. Jennifer hated doing dishes by hand. For as long as she could remember her family had had a dishwasher. *Yuck!*

After washing a few more glasses, she turned from the sink and looked at the TV. "Another night with the boob tube and me," she said to no one. "How can two people who believe in marriage and love and sex be so miserable?" She shook her head. "Well, here you are, twenty years old and already talking to yourself. Forget this!" She threw the dishrag into the sudsy water. "Let's see how the real world lives." Plopping down in front of the TV, she tuned in "Dallas."

IF YOU WANT TO EXPLORE OTHER CHOICES JENNIFER COULD HAVE MADE, RETURN TO PAGE 12 OR 73.

■1 ERIC (cont. from page 96)

Eric has been unable to tell his mother and father what is bothering him, but his obvious depression and falling grades alerted them that Eric needed to talk to someone. They made an appointment for him with a Christian counselor. For their second appointment, the counselor asked Eric to meet him in the park.

"Do you often see your clients out here?" Eric asked. He liked Mr. Robinson. He had felt immediately accepted by him.

"No." The counselor laughed. "Just ones that can appreciate the beauty of being outdoors. Did you get your reading done?"

"I sure did. The material was really helpful," Eric admitted. "I guess I'd done a good job convincing myself I had to be gay."

"That you did!" Mr. Robinson walked over and sat on one of the park benches.

Eric looked around. Relieved that there was no one else in the area, he sat on the bench beside the counselor. The sun felt good on Eric's back and he began to relax.

"I've had clients who have decided they are gay because a homosexual has made a pass at them—or because their brother or sister or aunt is gay."

Eric tucked one foot under him. "Do most people go as far as I did and try it out?" he asked.

"Some do. Some don't. You made a mistake and you sinned. That's a fact." There was no condemnation in Mr. Robinson's tone. He was merely stating the obvious.

"You know," Eric said, "when I confessed my sin and asked forgiveness, it was like a big load was taken off my shoulders."

"But have you forgiven yourself?" Mr. Robinson asked point blank.

"I'm working on it. I've decided to quit comparing myself to the other guys. The Bible talks about all the bad things that happen to people when we do that. I think I learned my lesson." He picked up a small twig and began breaking off little pieces and tossing them across the sidewalk.

"I want you to keep being aware of the things you think about. Erotic fantasies are out."

Eric appreciated Mr. Robinson's frank guidelines. The counselor also taught him to be careful of the kinds of things he allowed himself to be exposed to. Eric knew he could go to him for correct information and instruction.

Eric never again participated in a homosexual act. As he matured, he gained confidence in his sense of manhood. He married in his thirties and became a good husband and father.

IF YOU WANT TO EXPLORE MORE OF ERIC'S POSSIBLE CHOICES, RETURN TO PAGE 18 OR 173.

THE GIFT OF SEX

Here's what's happening:

■ JASON: Jason is a little cautious about starting a relationship with Suzy. He has known only two kinds of Christians: those whose faith seemed to make no impact on their life, and those who acted "holier-than-thou" and never seemed to have any fun, especially any fun having to do with sex. So he thought the Bible's message was: sex is bad, dirty, and nasty—save it for someone you love.

■1 MICHELLE: It was fortunate for Michelle and Howard that they sought Christian therapy. After they learned the true meaning and purpose of sex, they could accept its use as a loving gift from an adoring Father.

Sex is a gift? Let's explore that thought, and then continue with Jason's and Michelle's stories.

The Gift of Sex

Once upon a time in a kingdom long ago, a handsome lord fell in love with a beautiful lady and married her.

A mighty king ruled over the land. He was a good king, the very best. And wanting only the best for his people, he gifted them with presents uniquely suited for them. He never demanded obedience. He didn't have to. People loved him because they were loved by him. Those who didn't love him were known as blockheads for their inability to see what was clearly in their best interest.

To commemorate the special love of the lord and lady, the king sent them a gift that was designed to keep their love alive and fresh for a lifetime—the gift of sex.

A book of instruction was included. It contained only two rules. The first was that they were not to share the gift of sex with anyone except each other. It was theirs alone—nontransferable. The second was that whenever they used the gift, it was to be by mutual agreement.

At first, things were wonderful. They took out their gift regularly and shared their bodies without shame and with joyful passion. Each communicated to the other exactly what and how much of the gift he or she wanted. Their happiness grew, for each time they shared the gift they felt more like they were "one." Several years slipped by, and the lady conceived a child.

One day an advisor to the lord suggested that now that the honeymoon was over and a child was expected, it would be in the lord's best interest as a family man, to give more attention to concerns of the manor.

Following his advice, the lord began to work extra hours. Often he was too preoccupied to share the gift, but not wanting his lady to know he did not feel like sharing, he discovered he could pick a fight with her right before they were to bring out the gift. She would get angry and say she didn't feel like sharing the gift after all, and he could act hurt.

After the baby was born, there were times when the lady was simply too tired for the gift. She no longer told him what part of the gift she wanted. She left it up to him to decide. Her disinterest made him try harder to force her to enjoy the gift as they once had. A strange transformation took place. Whereas before, the other's pleasure had been as important as his or her *own, now each resented not getting exactly the part of the gift desired.*

Having misplaced the instructions, they sought help from their advisors. Their problem, the advisors said, was that they simply did not have enough rules for the gift's proper use. The advisors came up with the following:

1. *The gift should be used as little as possible, preferably on Saturday night.*
2. *It must be treated with utmost dignity: little talking and definitely no moans.*
3. *Only specified parts were to go in specified places. Violations would be considered perversions.*

After a while, the lord and lady rarely brought the gift out. It was too painful.

One day, feeling despair and missing the joy he used to derive from the gift of sex, the lord decided to share the gift with someone else. When his lady found out, they both understood why the instructions had expressly forbidden such behavior. They despaired over whether they would ever again be able to enjoy their gift.

One of their children asked about the gift once.

"Oh, that. We think it was a present from the Prince of Darkness," the lord and lady replied. Neither of them could recall that the special gift was from the Great King.

How tragic! But how similar to the Christian experience with the gift of sex. What started out as *good* has, for many people, become *bad* . Sex has caused them great pain and confusion. They have misplaced the instructions and added baggage the sex life was never meant to carry. With no way to check out misinformation and considering the silence on sexual issues from the pulpit, many mistakenly assume that sex is no longer under God's jurisdiction.

The Bible, however, contains a how-to book on sex called Song of Solomon, which demonstrates that sex is to be a joyful, passionate, bonding experience that lasts for a lifetime. Yet Song of Solomon is probably the most undertaught book there is. In the past, scholars were so sure that God could not have been talking about the sexual love between a man and a woman that they determined the book was an allegory of God's love for Israel or Christ's love for the Church. That is certainly a legitimate interpretation, but Song of Solomon is also an erotic love poem— right in the middle of the Bible.

It is the long-lost instruction manual. It contains a wealth of information about premarital courtship, but its main focus is the pleasure derived from marital love. Both the man and the woman eagerly anticipate sharing their bodies with one another. Each clearly communicates what he or she wants, all the while expressing love for the other by reaching out to fulfill the other's needs. The book also describes and resolves a sexual problem. Sections of the poem remind couples of the important elements of a good sexual relationship in marriage: romance, creativity, avoidance of boredom, the use of all senses in lovemaking, and thinking of the spouse in both loving and arousing ways.

Because it was written long ago, some of the symbolism is hard for twentieth-century minds to understand. You have to wonder whether "your hair is like a flock of goats" or "your teeth are like a flock of sheep" are really compliments! A good commentary or study book that explains the use of the metaphors and unusual words can be most helpful!

God has given us a free gift, a gift of pleasure that is unsurpassable if used according to the instructions. When we misuse the gift, however, or forget who gave it to us, it becomes a shadow of what it was meant to be. If you still doubt that the gift of sex is gift of pleasure, read the following scriptures:

John 10:10: "I have come that they may have life, and have it to the full."

1 Timothy 4:4: "For everything God created is good, and nothing is to be rejected if it is received with thanksgiving."

What happens next?

■   JASON (cont. from page 101)
Jason, like many people including Christians, had never bothered to look at the source, the Bible, to see what God's

message about sex was. He depended on "what everyone knows." Strangely attracted to Suzy, his feelings are mixed. What should he do?

■1. Even though he thinks the Christian motto is: "If it feels good, *don't* do it," Jason asks Suzy out. She just looks too good to pass up. After all, he's been fantasizing about her every day anyway—and maybe she'll give in, if he plays his cards right.
GO TO PAGE 26 AND LOOK FOR ■1

■2. Jason definitely wants to date Suzy, even though she is clearly not "one of those girls." He knows she won't give in to him—in fact, even though he finds her very attractive, it doesn't seem to be her sex appeal that is attracting him. There's just something about her.
GO TO PAGE 107 AND LOOK FOR ■2

■1 MICHELLE (cont. from page 101)
Several years later. . .
As Michelle finished giving her children their baths and got them ready for bed, she smiled at their stalling tactics.

Teddy was in one of his nonstop-questions moods. "Mom, why doesn't Amy have a penis like me?" he asked.

Michelle's heart pounded. It was hard to answer her forever-curious three-year-old's frank questions on sex. She swallowed hard. "Because you are a boy, and every boy has a penis so he can urinate and someday give his wife a baby if they want one. Penises can feel good too. Little girls have vulvas. Within it they have a separate area for urination, for giving birth to a baby, and for pleasure."

"Well, I think mine is better," he replied.

Michelle could barely keep a straight face. Pulling his snuggliest pair of PJs from his dresser, she helped him slip into them. "I'm glad you like your body," she said, giving him a big hug. "It is just right for you. And Amy's body is just right for her because she is a girl."

Michelle was determined to be an "askable" parent. Her

children would not be victims if she had anything to do with it. They were already learning that their bodies were special, private, and personal.

Teddy gave her another hug and jumped into bed. "Good night, Mommy. I love you," he said. Pulling his covers up to his chin, he cocked his head and smiled at her sweetly. "But how does a TV work?"

This time she laughed aloud. "Enough already! We'll deal with TV sets tomorrow," she replied. "It's lights out for you, buddy!" Giving him a kiss, she started out of the room, then hesitated at the light switch, reminding him to talk to Jesus.

A few seconds later Michelle turned off the light and eased into the hall. Leaning against the wall, she thanked the Lord for blessing her with two beautiful and healthy children. *And thanks, Lord, for the openness Howard and I are developing with your gift of sex,* she added. *It is protecting our children from abuse and helping us remain sensitive to potential sexual problems in our relationship.*

"Mom," a small voice from the bedroom said, "how does Jesus hear me?"

IF YOU WANT TO EXPLORE OTHER CHOICES MICHELLE COULD HAVE MADE, RETURN TO PAGE 16 OR 150.

THE METAMORPHOSIS

Here's what's happening:

■2 JASON: Jason had heard many "true" things about Christians and sex that had turned out to be lies. Now Suzy told him about her "Savior." What possible thing could a great girl like Suzy need saving from—other than perhaps Jason himself?

◯1 JASON: A few perceptive friends saw a change in Jason. He was not the same carefree guy he had always been. The locker room jokes didn't seem so funny anymore. Jason was mourning the loss of a son or daughter he never saw and hadn't planned on. Maybe he was going crazy. It didn't make sense.

Craig, the friend who had invited him over to watch the "Why Wait?" TV special, approached him after class. "Jason, you seem down. Why don't you come over after school? We can talk or listen to tapes, or whatever."

Jason started to say no, but something prompted him to say yes instead. He needed a friend.

1

MICHELLE: Living life like there is no God is living in a pretend world. Michelle thought she could find happiness by taking her life into her own hands and making sure it progressed the way she wanted it to. She tried playing God, but it didn't make her happy. Actually, it led her to bring another life into the world. The way things turned out she couldn't be a god of happiness to her baby either. Now there were two people whose lives weren't turning out they way they were supposed to!

Both Jason and Michelle find themselves in situations beyond their power to control; they'd give anything to change the way their life is turning out, but they don't know what to do. We'll return to their stories as soon as we've examined one alternative that's always there—for anyone.

The Metamorphosis

Both my kids have brought home D's in biology at various times. It makes me furious. I can't understand it. You see, I used to *teach* biology! To make matters worse, they both hate biology. After the appropriate threats, pleas, and tears, they managed to pass with some degree of respectability. But, I simply could not believe that my own offspring weren't as enraptured as I about the glorious ways of nature.

Take the butterfly, for instance. What a story! A simple, nondescript egg develops into this ugly creature that only a mother could love (come to think of it, even its mother splits). And through an amazing transformation, it becomes a thing of beauty any mother would be proud to love.

In my first year of teaching I asked on a test what the four stages of a butterfly's life cycle were. One of the students, undoubtedly one whose mother was a former biology teacher, answered, "The four stages of a butterfly are, front stage, back stage, left stage and right stage."

In reality, the first stage is the egg. Looking at it, you would never know there could be so much potential in something so little and nondescript.

Once the egg is hatched, the larva of the butterfly becomes an incredibly selfish and efficient eating machine. It devours many times its weight daily and can destroy any garden, crop, or tree its mother has deposited it on. Its eating becomes a frenzied, round-the-clock search for fulfillment—somewhat like modern-day teen-agers, who many parents say are on a continual search for anything and everything that will satisfy their cravings.

While this stage is appropriate and normal in the life cycle of the butterfly (and apparently the human), to choose to remain a larva means missing out on better days to come. The butterfly has no choice. It progresses to its next stage automatically. Some humans, however, decide to live at this stage forever. They spend their entire lives indulgently striving to "grab all the gusto" as the commercial says.

The butterfly, at this stage just an overweight worm, instinctively looks for a sheltered spot, hangs its head down and becomes very quiet. It spins a cocoon around its gluttonous body, and from the outside nothing seems to be going on. Inside there is a frenzy of activity—tissues are changing, hormones are flowing, a "metamorphosis" is taking place. When the cocoon finally splits, that selfish, single-minded, over-stuffed larva has transformed into its final adult stage and emerges as a beautiful butterfly.

No longer is it just an eating machine. The butterfly is adapted for participation in life beyond itself. It is able to reproduce and continue the species. Even its eating habits benefit other areas of nature because it spreads pollen from flower to flower.

You can undergo a metamorphosis too, but you must choose to do so. As with the butterfly, change often begins when you hang your head down and get quiet. Others often don't notice the equally dramatic transformation going on inside, at least in the beginning. But soon your new life shows no signs of selfishness and over-indulgence as you adapt to seeing beyond yourself to the needs and concerns of others and future generations.

Our cocoon, the site of transformation, is not a place but a person. New and beautiful lives begin when "larva" decide they've

109

had enough of their "grub-like" ways and choose to become an "adult." God could have made the change an automatic process, but he didn't. He gave each person the option to choose at what stage they want to live.

Why would he do such a thing? Because God created human beings to have a personal relationship with him.

"You made all the delicate, inner parts of my body, and knit them together in my mother's womb. Thank you for making me so wonderfully complex!" (Ps. 139:13-14 TLB).

He loves each person and wants every life to count.

"For God loved the world so much that he gave his only Son so that anyone who believes in him shall not perish but have eternal life" (John 3:16 TLB).

He wants everyone to know him.

"And this is the way to have eternal life—by knowing you, the only true God, and Jesus Christ, the one you sent to earth!" (John 17:3 TLB).

Why don't some people see any value in developing to the "adult" stage where God promises joy, peace, and life eternal? Choosing to remain a "larva," instead of developing into all a person can be is sin, and it keeps us from having a relationship with God.

"Knowing what is right to do and then not doing it is sin" (James 4:17 TLB).

"All have sinned; all fall short of God's glorious ideal" (Rom. 3:23 TLB).

Because God loves each individual, he provided a way for sins to be forgiven and a personal relationship to be restored.

"I am the Way—yes, and the Truth and the Life. No one can get to the Father except by means of me" (John 14:6 TLB).

Jesus died to pay the penalty for your sins, so that you might be forgiven.

"He died once for the sins of all us guilty sinners, although he himself was innocent of any sin at any time, that he might bring us safely home to God" (1 Pet. 3:18 TLB).

Then he rose from the dead to prove he could give people eternal life.

"Christ died for our sins just as the Scriptures said he would. . . he was buried. . .three days afterwards he arose from the grave just as the prophets foretold. . .he was seen by more than five hundred Christian brothers at one time. . ." (1 Cor. 15:3–6 TLB).

Metamorphosis actually takes place when you trust in Christ as Savior and Lord.

"Because of his kindness you have been saved through trusting Christ. And even trusting is not of yourselves; it too is a gift from God. Salvation is not a reward for the good we have done, so none of us can take any credit for it" (Eph. 2:8–9 TLB)

When you trust in Christ, you begin a lifelong relationship with God, and he commits himself to you.

"And now just as you trusted Christ to save you, trust him, too, for each day's problems. . . .See that you go on growing in the Lord, and become strong and vigorous in the truth" (Col. 2:6–7 TLB).

Trusting Christ makes you beautiful from the inside out, like the butterfly.

"When someone becomes a Christian he becomes a brand new person inside. He is not the same any more. A new life has begun!" (2 Cor. 5:17 TLB).

(This discussion was adapted from *Your Most Important Relationship*, Campus Crusade for Christ, Int'l., San Bernardino, CA 92414.)

What happens next?

■2 JASON (cont. from page 107)

"Hi, Suzy." Jason tried to look casual when he "accidentally" bumped into her after fifth period. Discovering her pattern had taken three days, cost two hamburgers (a bribe to a guy in some of her classes), and a detention for being late to his next class. But when she flashed her bright smile his way, it was all worthwhile.

"Well, hi, Jason," Suzy replied. "I didn't know you had a class over here."

Jason hoped the heat he felt creeping up his neck was not sending out red flags saying *Look at me! Look at me!* "Hey," he managed. "I wondered if you'd like to go out Friday night." *Might as well get this over fast,* he thought.

"I appreciate the invitation. . ." Suzy hesitated a moment.

Uh-oh, here it comes. Jason forced his smile, waiting for the gentle letdown. As he walked beside her, he picked up his pace and began to readjust his books.

"Please don't take this wrong, but I make it a rule not to really date anyone who doesn't share my faith. Do you mind if I ask what you believe about Jesus Christ, Jason?" she asked.

They were just outside her classroom now, and Jason wasn't sure what to do. *Oh well,* he thought, *better to have loved and lost. . .* He shrugged. "I don't know," he said. "I guess I've never really thought about it."

"Tell you what." She was still smiling. "Let's meet Friday after school for a Coke, and I'll tell you what *I* believe."

Jason wasn't at all sure he wanted to hear what she believed, but any excuse to be with her sounded good to him. "You're on," he said quickly before she disappeared into the classroom. But even though he had to sprint to make it to his class on time, he didn't care.

That innocent Coke date changed Jason's life. Before it was over he agreed to go with her to her church's youth group—anything for a few moments more of her company!

There, a whole new world opened for Jason. It was scary but he couldn't seem to stay away. He and Suzy continued to hit it off, but being with her was no longer his only motivation. Within a month he accepted Christ as his personal Savior.

GO TO PAGE 54 AND LOOK FOR ■2

01 JASON (cont. from page 107)

"I can see you're really suffering, Jason," Craig said sympathetically.

Jason hadn't intended to share what was on his mind, but here he was, crying like a baby in Craig's kitchen. He would never live this down. "You probably think I'm a real jerk." He searched Craig's face for any sign of rejection but could find none. "It seems so stupid. Why should I care? She doesn't. I just feel depressed."

"Actually, I like the guy you are right now—the one who hurts and cares—a whole lot more than the one I usually see."

Jason looked up, startled. Craig had never participated in the put-downs and exaggerations so common among the team. Everyone liked him but he was "different." *Oh, yeah,* he thought, *I remember now. He's a Christian.* "I thought most of you Christians hated abortions," he said.

"We don't take life lightly, Jason," Craig replied. "If it's OK to kill a baby this week, maybe next week it'll be OK to kill anyone over forty, or those under five, or football teams!"

Jason smiled. "I see what you mean." Unable to get the brochure picture of a tiny baby's dismembered body out of his mind, he shuddered. "What do you think happens to babies who are aborted?" he asked.

"Most Christians believe that since unborn babies are innocent and God is a loving God, those aborted babies are whole and living with him. But you shouldn't take my word for it. We can look up some Scriptures that will help you see why we believe that." Craig headed into his room and was back in a flash with his own well-worn Bible and one for Jason.

For the next hour, Craig patiently pointed out Scriptures that revealed God's love for us all, including Jason's unborn baby—and Jason himself.

Jason just shook his head. "That I can't believe. How can God love me after everything I've done?"

Craig sat back in his chair and looked silently at Jason for a long time. Then he said, "Have you ever wondered why God allowed Jesus to die on that cross when he could have sent a whole army of angels to rescue him? It was because God wanted to be able to love you, despite whatever you've done."

Jason was ready to listen. He became a new person in Christ that day.

Gradually, his old behaviors slipped away. He never looked on girls the same way again. No longer seeing sex as just a recreational activity for physical pleasure, he respected it as a sacred gift by which life begins.

He found comfort in knowing that someday he would see his child in heaven. Until then, he or she was safe in the arms of Jason's heavenly father, his closest friend.

IF YOU WOULD LIKE TO EXPLORE OTHER CHOICES JASON COULD HAVE MADE, GO TO PAGE 14 OR 138.

O1 MICHELLE (cont. from page 108)

As Michelle sat on a couch in one of the counseling rooms at a church-operated center for teen mothers, she smiled at her sleeping baby in the infant seat between her and her counselor, Mrs. Bradley. After her husband left her she began several weeks of counseling at the center and soon accepted the Lord Jesus Christ as her personal Savior. But the decision that brought her here today seemed even harder.

"Are you absolutely sure, Michelle?" Mrs. Bradley leaned a little closer to her.

Michelle nodded. "I've really prayed about this," she replied. "It's strange," she continued. "It's the most painful thing I've ever done, and yet I have peace about it. I know it's the right thing for April and for me."

Mrs. Bradley reached over and adjusted April's blanket. "It takes a lot of love to overlook your own needs and desires to do the best for someone else," she said. "Placing your baby up for adoption is an act of love and courage."

"After my husband left I really thought I could manage on my own," Michelle admitted. "But that night when she wouldn't stop crying and I threw her down on the bed—"

"That's when you found our number in the phone book, right?" Mrs. Bradley asked.

"Yes, I knew I had to do something. I love April so much. I would never want to hurt her. But I almost did!" Michelle rocked the infant seat gently. "I was scared."

"Thank the Lord she wasn't hurt."

"You can say that again," Michelle replied. "I heard something in our Bible study the other day that really helped. The teacher made the point that when people don't choose God's best, any solution they use to 'fix' the problem automatically starts out being second best."

"That's so true, Michelle. We can't go back to the best if we've passed it up and chosen another way. We can, however, be forgiven for refusing to take the best." Mrs. Bradley squeezed Michelle's hand. "God will honor your faith by supplying April with a new family to love her," she assured Michelle. "And he will make sure that your life has meaning and purpose, too."

GO TO PAGE 19 AND LOOK FOR ○1

AGAINST HER WILL IS AGAINST THE LAW

Here's what's happening:

✱✱1 JASON: Cathy's message has been loud and clear—or so it seems to Jason. She's been hot for him, and he isn't about to miss an opportunity. And if she protests a little, that's just part of the game, isn't it?

We'll continue Jason's story as soon as we explore that crucial question.

Against Her Will Is Against the Law

When I was a little girl, I grew up hearing about Little Red Riding Hood, Sleeping Beauty, and the Three Little Pigs. I also learned that being a female meant being vulnerable. Things could happen to girls. I lived with an unnamed dread that catastrophe could be around the next corner.

What do fairy tales and rape have in common? You'd be surprised. Most every fairy tale presents a picture of a beautiful but helpless female who will be safe as long as she waits (or sleeps) patiently or doesn't veer off the path. Her protector and defender is a strong male who appears on the scene just in the nick of time!

Contrast the female characters with their male counterparts: strong huntsmen, beautiful princes, dastardly "wolves" who prey on the innocent. You will notice that those three little (male) pigs were not afraid of the "Big Bad Wolf," and neither was a little boy named Peter when he encountered one.

This comparison doesn't mean that in the real world men and boys don't have to worry about being overpowered and raped. Rape of men occurs, but cases are rarely taken to court. Instead, the male rape victim most often suffers in silence, covers his fears with bravado, or tragically acts out his feelings of anger, rage, and frustration by victimizing someone else. Good, brave men, after all, are strong and in charge.

Traditionally our society has portrayed two messages to females: (1) women should passively wait for a man to activate their sexual desires, and (2) straying off the path of expected behavior gets you into trouble. This mentality makes a woman vulnerable to a rapist—especially if she knows him.

For many women, to be feminine means to be kind, to take orders from men, and to be accommodating. In a sense women are trained to be rape victims. One convicted rapist told how he picked his victims: Approaching women with arms full of packages, he asked for either the time or a match. If the woman tried to accommodate him, he had his victim. He knew she would do whatever he asked.

A study conducted at UCLA in 1980 revealed that half the male students would force a woman into a sexual act if they knew they would not be punished. Do they think they are rescuing women—like Cinderella or Snow White—or do they simply think it is a masculine right?

A three-year Kent State University study of 6,200 male and female students from 32 campuses, found that 15% of the women had been raped, over half of them by people they knew. Another researcher estimates that 20% of the college women she surveyed had been victims, mostly of date rape—some before and some after entering college.

Date rape occurs most frequently in the 15-to-24 age group. Victimizers are more sexually active than other males and may have a history of antisocial behavior. Victims often fail to admit having been raped, and only 5% report the incident to the police. Many are too stunned to believe such a thing could have happened, and they fail to seek professional help.

Occasionally, date rape occurs after the victim has taken drugs or alcohol, making the whole incident one cloudy bit of terror. Under such circumstances, their testimony would have little chance of standing up in court.

The victim inevitably endures a case built upon her "contributory" behavior. Did the woman who allowed the handyman into her house for a drink of water contribute to her rape? Did the girl who wore a skirt slightly too short? How about the college girl who accepted a ride home from the library in a classmate's car? A study done by the National Commission on the Causes and Prevention of Violence found that rape victims contributed less to their victimization than victims of any other kinds of violent crimes.

Scripture mentions several incidents of rape, always with dire consequences. The most important passage has to be 1 Thessalonians 4:6, which says that no one is to take advantage of another sexually. To do so is to reject God.

Only those who are ignorant suggest that a victim of date rape simply "got what she asked for" or "got scared and changed her mind" or "really wanted it all along." In court, against her will is against the law.

What happens next?

∗∗1 JASON (cont. from page 116)

"Look, Cathy, I managed to get us a couple of beers."

Cathy ushered Jason into her deserted house. Every other family member had gone out for the evening. They were completely alone.

Time flew as they watched TV, had their beers, and talked. Jason enjoyed the sight of Cathy's skirt barely covering the necessary parts when she sat down. He reached over and kissed her longingly.

"Oh, Cathy, if you only knew what you do to me," he mumbled as he moved her further down on the couch.

Cathy felt a tingly feeling both in her head from the beer and in her genitals as he ran his hand over the front of her skirt. *It's neat being grown up,* she thought to herself.

Suddenly she felt Jason's hand up her blouse, taking off her bra. "No, Jason," she whispered.

Typical female, Jason thought. *Has to play the innocent.* He slid out of his shirt.

"Maybe we'd better cool it a little," Cathy protested, her head clearing quickly.

But there was no stopping Jason. "Hey, no teasing, all right? I know you like me." He held her—tightly.

Frightened, Cathy began fighting wildly, pushing and shoving, but her maneuvers to get out from under him only helped Jason get a firmer hold. She pleaded with him to stop, but soon they were on the floor.

Seconds later, Cathy felt a sharp pain. She screamed. "Please, Jason, please don't! I've never—" The tears flowed.

The scream had gotten his attention, and now there was blood. Cathy was a virgin. "Why didn't you tell me you'd never done it?" he yelled. "It's your fault, parading around like you knew what you're doing!"

Jason felt angry, but he also felt like crying. Silently he helped Cathy up, got dressed, and went home.

GO TO PAGE 91 AND LOOK FOR ⁂1

AND BABY
MAKES TWO

Here's what's happening:

∗∗2 JASON: Cathy and Jason did not use birth control. Like most teens who begin a sexual relationship, they didn't figure she could get pregnant the first few times, and they didn't want to ruin the mood. Jason didn't worry because he didn't think it was his responsibility. Guess what? Unprotected intercourse is how babies are made.

We'll return to Jason's story as soon as we've examined what that means.

And Baby Makes Two

Of the one million teenage pregnancies annually, 400,000 are aborted, 470,000 result in live births, and the rest are miscarried or stillborn. The United States has the highest rate of teenage pregnancy of any developed country—double the nearest contender.

By far the greatest tragedy of these appalling statistics is the overwhelming hardships that individual teens and their children must face. Most teens who keep their babies are trapped in a cycle of poverty they rarely escape because of limited educational and employment opportunities.

Frustration and poor parental training result in a higher rate of child abuse. Pregnancy interrupts school, work goals, career plans, and the natural process of adolescence. Before a girl has finished or gotten used to the physical changes of her body and her budding sexuality, she is thrust into adulthood.

Media stars leave the impression that single parenthood is somehow chic. In reality it's an eighteen-year nontransferable commitment to sleepless nights, hundreds of dirty diapers, overwhelming responsibility, and a tiny but growing person who takes more love that he or she gives.

Mature adults are frequently overwhelmed with the task. A kid with a kid is bound to be discouraged once reality sets in. At that point our social organizations try to help change the usual sad scenario so that both mother and child can feel hopeful.

Only one out of five pregnant teens marries the father of her child. Of those who do not abort their babies, few release them for adoption. God's plan for a two-parent, stable home is considered less important than it was in the past. But the healthiest children are found in such homes. Society says that stable homes no longer need the presence of two sexes. Though this may be an attempt to justify the many divorced households, it is a lie.

Emotional and social complications are not the only problems. A young girl who becomes sexually active and has more than one sexual partner, may double her risk of developing cervical dysplasia (precancer) or invasive cancer. And the earlier a girl begins sexual activity, the more partners she is apt to have.

Four partners increase her chance of developing Pelvic Inflammatory Disease (PID) threefold. Increased risk is not limited to the girl's behavior, either. If her boyfriend has had four sexual partners, he increases his virginal girlfriend's chance of developing cancer by as much as ten percent.

Because young girls tend to deny that they could be pregnant, they put off getting medical care. Those having abortions, get them later in their pregnancies, and there is an increased rate of injury to the cervix. Since the pelvis has not completed its growth, there is increased hypertension (high blood pressure) due to pregnancy and cephalopelvic disproportion (in which the head of the baby is larger in proportion to the pelvis than normal).

Teen mothers are:

—15% more likely to get toxemia, a life-threatening complication of pregnancy that involves retention of poisonous fluids
—92% more likely to become anemic
—23% more likely to give birth prematurely or have a low-weight baby
—twice as likely to die.

Early prenatal care can minimize many of these problems. Lack of good care leads to complications like low birth weight and difficulties at birth, which lead to a higher death rate. Inadequate care after childbirth, often due to lack of money or transportation, often results in developmental and learning difficulties.

And without counseling and support, the odds of a young girl getting pregnant again are high because the contributing social and educational factors haven't changed.

Pregnancy never proves someone's masculinity or womanliness. It never guarantees you someone to love who will love you back. Young people are wisest to consider taking on this responsibility only when the parental load can be carried by two committed, loving people, who are mature enough to make the sacrifices and compromises necessary for a child's healthy development. Unfortunately, our society makes it easier for boys and girls to become parents than to get a driver's license.

What happens next?

**2 JASON (cont. from page 120)

"But Cathy," Jason protested, "this can't be. You told me it was your safe time."

"I thought it was, Jason." Cathy could barely get the words out. "I guess I miscalculated."

"But you can't get pregnant if you didn't have an orgasm." Jason didn't know who he was trying to convince: himself or Cathy. "This wasn't supposed to happen." He shook his head, realizing how stupid that sounded.

"Well, it did," Cathy said bitterly. "The doctor is sure. Facts are facts."

After Cathy's announcement, the rest of the day went downhill from there.

His dad wasn't any help at all. "What do you mean *you* got a girl pregnant? It could be *anybody's* baby!" he shouted. "You don't have to take the blame."

Cathy's father turned homicidal. "Get that creep out of my sight before I kill him!" he yelled.

As Jason walked home through the woods, he couldn't handle any more. "Why me?" he cried. "What do I do now?"

GO TO PAGE 124 AND LOOK FOR ⁂2

THE BIOLOGICAL FATHER

Here's what's happening:

✱✱2 JASON: Jason realizes that two wrongs don't make a right; he knows that marrying Cathy would be a mistake. Even Cathy doesn't push for it. But the baby—the baby is his own flesh and blood. He can't just walk out on the baby. But what rights does he have?

Let's talk about it, and then we'll return to Jason's story.

The Biological Father

Only five percent of pregnant teenage girls marry the father of their child. There's a common belief that most teen fathers are happy to be off the hook, and having "proven" their manhood, they split. In truth, many young fathers willingly concede that impregnation doesn't make them a father. Parenting does.

Though they are few, counseling programs that teach parental skills and provide job training find eager participants. Follow-up results are encouraging. In one program, after two years, 82% had daily contact with their children, 74% helped financially, and 90%

maintained a relationship with the mother. Apparently, young men are willing to be a part of the child's upbringing if they get the help they need. Without it, they tend to fall into the I-think-I'll-split category.

Some teen fathers want to do the right thing, but they often complicate their mistake by quitting school to get a job. Ultimately, they have lower incomes, less education, and more children than young men who stay in school. Dropping out becomes a terrible trap.

If they haven't had a good father model, this also frustrates their good intentions. Many times their own dads have been absent emotionally or physically. How can they know how to be a good father if they haven't seen one in action? And there is greater risk of an unplanned pregnancy among young people whose parents experienced one.

In some regions, fathering a baby may offer status if life doesn't seem to offer much else. More often, the girl's family blames the boy for what has happened and tries to keep him out of the way: "Haven't you done enough already?"

Most young fathers are treated as an outsider in the events of pregnancy. Friends may desert or tease them. Almost all defer plans and dreams and begin adult routines of balancing night or vocational school, jobs, and baby care. Friday nights at the game, leisure time to just goof off, and childhood become things of the past.

Determining fatherhood isn't usually difficult. In some states if an unwed father admits his paternity or at least doesn't deny the assumption that he is the father, he is legally considered to be so. Tests that match genetic markers found in the parent and child are 95% accurate. While required if the mother applies for welfare benefits, they may also be important for inheritance purposes, social security, support, custody, and visitation.

Child custody is based on an 1881 Kansas Supreme Court decision that set the standard as what is in the best interest of the child. In the past, that almost always meant giving custody to the mother. But today the father who feels the best interest of the child is with him, can legally apply for custody.

The unmarried father may be allowed visitation if that is considered in the best interest of the child, if he has acknowledged paternity, or if he has demonstrated financial support, concern, and love according to the court criteria.

On the whole, the unwed father has very little control over what happens. In some states the child's last name must be the mother's. Other states allow a change of name almost at whim. But there is no guarantee the child will carry the father's name throughout his or her life.

What disturbs many teenage fathers who care about their child, however, is that the girl can abort without the father's permission. She can also relinquish the child for adoption over his objections. He can petition the court for custody, but he must be able to show that he is well qualified to care for the child—a near impossible task for a teenage boy. Usually, if there is a battle over custody or relinquishment, the girl simply keeps the baby and/or moves to a new area. If she remarries, her new husband can adopt her child quite easily in some areas of the country.

Becoming a biological father is no guarantee that a young man will have the opportunity to be a real father. With all the concerns of the pregnancy, the teen father's needs are shoved aside. Yet the father's willingness and desire to take responsibility reflects on God's design that parenting be a two-sex responsibility that extends beyond the planting of the seed to include its nurturing. Only then can healthy development be achieved.

What happens next?

**2 JASON (cont. from page 124)

As Jason lay on his bed in the dark, there were no sounds. The stereo, almost always blaring when he was in his room, sat silent.

"Jason!" His dad's booming voice carried up the stairs.

Hearing footsteps coming toward him, Jason rolled over, his back to the door, and pulled the pillow around his ears. *Just go away*, he thought.

The door swung open. "Jason, your mom told me the good news!" he crowed.

Jason ignored him.

"What's the matter, boy? Forget to pay your electrical bill?" As Dad flipped on the light, Jason rolled over and sat on the edge of his bed. Dad grinned broadly. "That little slut and her family have moved, and there's no forwarding address. You lucked out, kid!" He looked at Jason and frowned. "Why the long face, son? You should be celebrating!"

Jason groaned and rolled back on his bed. "Dad, I'll never see my kid."

Incredulous, Dad shook his head slowly. "Jason, where were you when they handed out brains?" he asked. "Now that you're off the hook, you can go on to college, just like you planned. You're free—no child support."

Jason got up, looked straight at his dad, and gathered all the courage he could muster. "But it's *my kid* Dad," he said. "I wanted to take care of it. I was just beginning to look forward to having a son or daughter of my own. I didn't want Cathy to have to face this alone."

"I'll never understand you, Jason," his dad said with disgust. "You're free as a bird." He turned and walked out of the room.

Jason didn't feel free as a bird. He never saw or heard from Cathy again and never even found out whether the baby was a boy or a girl. He knew, though, that the memory of what had happened would haunt him for the rest of his life.

IF YOU WANT TO EXPLORE OTHER CHOICES JASON COULD HAVE MADE, RETURN TO PAGE 14 OR 65.

LIFE BEFORE BIRTH: FEARFULLY AND WONDERFULLY MADE

Here's what's happening:

○1 JASON: At first Jason denies that it could be his fault, but Charlotte convinces him that he has to be the father. She says she wants an abortion and needs him to help her arrange and pay for it. Jason agrees that it's the only way out. He'll find a place for her to go. He looks in the phone book under Unplanned Pregnancy.

○2 MICHELLE: Michelle was overwhelmed by the pressures of her crisis pregnancy. Maybe her friends were right. An abortion would be the "simplest" solution.

Jason and Michelle have incredibly difficult decisions to make. We'll continue their stories as soon as we consider some of the information they'll need to make that decision.

Life Before Birth: Fearfully and Wonderfully Made

My husband is an obstetrician/gynecologist. In his work he sees many women who have had abortions. Typically, as he is

128

taking a medical history, he must ask about previous pregnancies. Inevitably, if the woman has had an abortion, she responds by lowering her voice and dropping her eyes—no matter what her religious persuasion or feelings about terminating pregnancies.

The year 1988 marked the fifteenth anniversary of legalized abortions in the United States (*Roe v. Wade*, 1973). Every professional conference on counseling I have attended in the last few years has had at least one presentation on some aspect of abortion. This "personal choice" issue is producing a groundswell of hurting men and women who have discovered that taking a life before birth has definite consequences.

In her book, *Will I Cry Tomorrow?* (Fleming H. Revell Company, Old Tappan, New Jersey, 1986), Susan Stanford writes of healing post-abortion trauma. The symptoms vary, and may occur immediately after the event or five to ten years hence. Some women experience depression around the anniversary of the abortion or the date the child would have been born. Others complain of a generalized depression or unhappiness plus all the usual symptoms of grieving (crying, sadness, anger, withdrawal). Some women are aware that their problems are related to the abortion while others fail to make the connection.

The healing process requires first a realization that there are unresolved issues surrounding the abortion, then a review of the details and emotions that led to the decision. (If a person does not believe in God, a counselor might be able to help him or her live more comfortably with the abortion decision, but this is like putting a Band-aid on a surgical wound. True healing comes from God alone.)

Some Christian counselors use prayer and guided imagery to encourage healing. In this process, the woman seeking healing is asked to remember—to allow the Holy Spirit to bring to mind some aspect of the abortion. Remaining prayerful and with her eyes shut, she shares the scene with the counselor. The counselor encourages her to be aware of the feelings and emotions present at that time. Tears often flow freely as the woman relives the experience.

When the counselor senses that the time is right, the woman is asked to imagine, somewhere in the scene, a loving, forgiving, healing Jesus. "He is holding a baby in his arms. He is holding your baby," the counselor says. "And he loves her just as much as you would if she were right here in *your* arms." Then the counselor asks the woman to picture herself standing in front of him, looking into his forgiving eyes, becoming aware of the love he feels for her baby. "His death on the cross was for her, too," the counselor says, "so she, like us, is pure in his eyes."

Time passes as the woman carries on a conversation in her mind with Jesus, telling him her feelings and listening to his response. Often, this is a tearful time of silence. The counselor doesn't want to interrupt this personal journey and healing experience.

While still in a contemplative position with her eyes closed, the woman, when she is ready, shares with the counselor what has transpired. The counselor writes everything down so that the woman may reread her impressions later and continue to learn from them.

Finally they pray and thank God for each child who through abortion or miscarriage never makes it to this earth. Acknowledging that God loves every soul created, they commit the woman's baby to the Lord. If the woman has a sense of the baby's sex or has a name for the baby (often she does), they use it in their prayer as they dedicate the child for all eternity. Then they thank the Father for the love and protection of his presence. "We are thankful, Lord, that one day _____ and her baby will be joined together in heaven," the counselor prays.

Abortion is more than eliminating a few "cells." These women whose "simple" procedure has left them emotionally scarred and needing such therapeutic intervention proves it.

Indeed, with the technology of the 80s, few deny the humanity of even the youngest fetus. The argument is no longer, "Is this a person from conception?" but "Who is, and who is not, entitled to societal protection?"

Roe v. Wade essentially said that the law doesn't have to protect unborn babies because they are not persons in the whole sense. (Could the courts come to the same conclusion later about the handicapped or the senile elderly?) If unborn babies were considered full persons, they would be protected under the

Constitution which promises every person certain rights and equal protection under the law.

What does God think? He tells us we are created in *his image* . We are different from the animals. Human beings have been set apart (Gen. 1:26). We were made differently (Gen. 2). And even after sin, God recognized our uniqueness (Gen. 9:6). Nowhere does God say that society's rejects are not made in his image. In fact, he seems to have a special place in his heart for the poor (Matt. 25:45), the children (Matt. 18:1-10), the handicapped (Zeph. 3:19), and the elderly (Lev. 19:32).

God doesn't pretend that unborn babies aren't people. In Jeremiah 1:5, he says, "Before I formed you in the womb I knew you, before you were born I set you apart." Scripture tells us things about other biblical characters before they were born, like Jacob and Esau, Ishmael, Samson, and Paul. And before John the Baptist was born, he jumped for joy in his mother's womb when Mary, who was pregnant with the Messiah, came to visit (Luke 1:41).

An unplanned pregnancy has no ideal solution. Sin never does. But post-abortion trauma victims have taught us that abortion is *not* the easy way out. We must be sensitive to those who do not know the truth or see no alternative. We can give them the loving support they need so other choices become realistic ones.

King David wrote about how much God has been involved in our lives even before we were born. Read the whole beautiful poem (Ps. 139) but note especially verses 13—16:

"For you created my inmost being; you knit me together in my mother's womb. I praise you because I am fearfully and wonderfully made; your works are wonderful, I know that full well. My frame was not hidden from you when I was made in the secret place. When I was woven together in the depths of the earth, your eyes saw my unformed body. All the days ordained for me were written in your book before one of them came to be."

Aren't we *all* fearfully and wonderfully made?

What happens next?

◯1 JASON (cont. from page 128)

Jason and Charlotte sat whispering in a back booth of their favorite hamburger place, their faces tense.

"Charlotte, this is wrong," Jason pleaded.

"It's not illegal," Charlotte shot back.

"I know it's not illegal. But look, just read these. I picked them up from a place I found in the phone book. The people there said they could help us. They can arrange for the baby to be adopted by a family that really wants it—"

"Oh, how sweet of them," she said sarcastically. "I can be a baby machine for someone else."

Jason bit his lip and tried to keep his voice down. "This is a real live baby we're talking about, not tickets to the homecoming dance."

"It is not a 'real live baby.' It's a bunch of cells."

"It *is* a real live baby, Charlotte," Jason insisted. "Just read the brochures. Look at these pictures. You'll see for yourself."

"It's not a person—but I am. I'm not going to ruin my life over a few minutes in the back seat of a car. Are you going to help me or not?"

"I'll marry you, Charlotte. Please don't get an abortion." Desperately, Jason grabbed her hand, hoping she could see how serious he was.

"I can't believe this. I don't *want* to marry you. I just want you to help me of a jam you helped me get into. If you won't help, forget it. I don't need you. My friends will pitch in for me."

They did. And Jason couldn't do a thing about it.

GO TO PAGE 107 AND LOOK FOR ◯1

◯2 MICHELLE (cont. from page 128)

Michelle's life was crumbling around her. The simple solution of abortion, now that it was done, had turned out to be enormously complicated and costly. Michelle needed help. A friend recommended a Christian counselor who was familiar with Post-Abortion Syndrome.

Maxine was an attractive woman in her early thirties, and her office felt comfortable, almost homey. "Hello, Michelle," the counselor greeted her warmly. "I'm glad you decided to come. You sounded rather hesitant on the phone."

Michelle took a seat in a rocker by the windows. "I almost didn't. I'm still not sure anyone can help me." The rocking chair creaked in a melodic rhythm.

"But someone can," Maxine replied. Before Michelle could ask who, she continued, "Tell me what led to your coming to see me."

"My husband left me," Michelle began, surprised at how safe she felt talking to Maxine. She hadn't really been open to anyone about her problem. *How can you,* she thought, *when your problem is that you killed your baby?* "We had some financial problems, and then I got pregnant. We couldn't afford a baby. We went to this clinic, and they said it wasn't a baby, just tissue. So we decided it was our only choice."

"Did you have doubts when you went to the clinic?" Maxine asked.

"To be honest, I was so confused and scared—and my husband said he would leave me if I didn't do it—it's almost like I couldn't think." She paused, stopping the rocker mid melody. "After we signed the papers at the clinic, I asked my husband if we were doing the right thing. But everybody was so cheery and sure, he told me it was just fine."

Maxine nodded sympathetically, then turned and reached for her Bible, laying it on her desk. "Did everything go as you had been told?"

"No, it was awful." Michelle looked down at her lap and began to rock again, double time now. "Something went wrong, and they had to use another procedure. I looked over and saw them matching up the parts of my baby to make sure they had all of it." Michelle's heart pounded but she didn't cry. She was all cried out. The sight of those tiny arms, legs, and other body parts still haunted her.

"How dreadful that must have been for you!" Maxine replied.

"I got hysterical," Michelle continued. "They had to give me a shot. My husband got so angry." She closed her eyes and swallowed hard. "He said I humiliated him."

"Did he leave you right away?"

Michelle shook her head. "A month or so later. He had said he'd leave me if I didn't get an abortion. But I did what he wanted and he left anyway." The rocker slowed to a moderate pace. "I have nightmares. I hate myself," she admitted. "Other people get pregnant at inconvenient times and don't do what I did."

Maxine picked up her Bible and leaned closer to Michelle. "I will not condone what you did or pretend it was not a sin. There are many issues we need to deal with, and we will. But, first, I'd like to show you some scriptures that help us understand where your baby is."

Michelle's heart skipped a beat. Her baby was still in existence? She hadn't dared hope. . .

GO TO PAGE 84 AND LOOK FOR ○2

WHY WAIT?

Here's what's happening:

○ JASON: Jason has had plenty of support for his attitude. Our society, his dad, and teammates have reinforced "getting it when you can." He has never heard anyone say anything different. Oh, those religious fanatics talk about God "zapping" you, but they're old-fashioned. Everyone knows God doesn't want you to have fun—so what? Why wait?

✱✱2 MICHELLE: Michelle sees no reason to wait until marriage for sexual relations. She feels good about being a somebody with the guys, even if it is a "used" somebody. She's getting what she needs now. The future can take care of itself.

Before we continue with Jason's and Michelle's stories, let's take a look at some things the two of them need to consider.

Why Wait?

Why do teenagers have sexual intercourse when they really don't want to? According to a recent survey, the girls answered:

—unable to say no when pressured
—afraid of losing boyfriend
—sense of obligation, a payback for cost of the date
—to show love or give reassurance
—being high on drugs or alcohol
—because it means a lot to the boy
—because I've led him on and don't want to seem like a tease
—being in a group where everyone else is doing it
—succumbing to persistent demands
—fear that not "going all the way" might mean losing the pleasures of petting
—to avoid fighting with boyfriend.

The boys answered:

—not to hurt the girl's feelings
—afraid she may think I don't like her
—to prove I am a man
—because it's expected
—being in a group where everyone else is doing it
—to have the experience, see what it's like
—being high on drugs or alcohol
—because the girl wants it
—nothing else to do on a date.

You can't miss the casualness of the reasons. Adolescents often engage in sex without giving it much thought or planning.[1]

By the teen years, both male and female bodies are capable of sexual intercourse. Minds and emotions might *not* be ready, but nobody worries about that detail. There seems no logical reason to wait. All systems are go!

BODY RARING TO GO + POTENTIAL RELATIONSHIP = SEX

or HORNINESS + LOVE = SEX

---

[1] Adapted from Barbara Herjanic, MD, Medical Aspects of Sexuality. "How Adolescents can Deal with Pressures to Engage in Sex," Vol.18 #6, June 84.

Abstaining doesn't make much sense to many, and most are convinced it is impossible, especially if you are in love. "Love" is supposed to justify what the Bible calls fornication (intercourse between two unmarried people).

Are there any good reasons for waiting? Other than God's ancient, seemingly arbitrary decree, if you are in love and your body is ready—*why wait*?

1. Physical love can be so pleasurable and all-consuming that your social development can come to a screeching halt. No more late nights with the girls or guys, no more chit-chatting at school. Couples in a sexual relationship want to be together all the time, and they plan their life accordingly. Socializing and learning about the world around them aren't as important anymore.

2. Maintaining a sexual relationship depends on sexual performance, because there is no permanent foundation. A broken relationship means "I didn't perform well." Such reasoning is wrong, but that doesn't repair the damaged self-image.

3. Sexually transmitted diseases (STDs) are rampant. Many can't be detected until a couple is tested to see why the woman can't get pregnant. Some STDs, like AIDS, lead to death. Others, like herpes, remain with a person for life.

4. Multiple partners increase the risk of reproductive complications (infertility, tubal pregnancy) and cancer (cervical).

5. An unplanned pregnancy is never easy to face. The options are dismal: abortion, interrupting school and social development to raise a child, giving up the child for adoption.

6. People who have sexual experiences before they marry bring extra baggage into the marriage that affects their relationship—that causes, for instance, comparisons, guilt, and low self-esteem.

7. Giving away "love" hurts. Making love is not like eating a Big Mac. You don't just walk away from the experience untouched. Taking someone's virginity is more than making love the first time because sex is more than the physical act. A person who has been raped is more than physically violated. No one ever forgets their first sexual experience.

8. Making love the first time breaks a barrier that becomes increasingly easier to cross.

9. People who have experienced intercourse before marriage, rob themselves of the enormous significance of giving themselves totally on their wedding night. A virgin's honeymoon is unique and unrepeatable. The wedding night symbolizes a significant change in the person's life. It indicates total commitment.

10. People who have had multiple sexual partners are more likely to have extramarital affairs. Sex has been cheapened, so giving it away means less to them.

11. Intense sexual involvement prevents a couple from discovering all the other aspects of their relationship.

12. Guilt over sexual activity can spoil a person's feelings about sex. When that person gets married, those feelings can weaken or destroy the marriage.

13. All sin separates us from God. Sexual sin makes a person feel uncomfortable with God.

14. God will judge our sexual sins. "Marriage is honorable among all, and the bed undefiled; but fornicators and adulterers God will judge (Heb. 13:4 NKJV).

15. God has not set up a standard no one can follow. He asks us to be sexually pure before marriage because He loves us and wants the best for us. The best means living life fully without guilt or worry about disease, pregnancy, and emotional baggage from sex out of its designed context.

God designed men and women to desire a physical relationship in marriage, and he has confidence in our ability to live our sexual life in a healthy way until then.

He could have designed other techniques: pollination (like flowers use), or cell division (like amoebas use), or cloning (like scientists have experimented with). But aren't you glad he didn't?

What happens next?

◯ JASON (cont. from page 135)
One of Jason's friends invites him to join his family for dinner. After dinner the whole family sits down and watches a "Why Wait?" TV special with Josh McDowell. Everyone

else seems to be impressed, and Jason actually allows himself to consider some of the reasons given for not having sex until marriage. The mood is temporary, however. Looking at how his present actions affects his future seems like an exercise in futility. The media's messages, "Grab all the gusto," "Do it now," and "Opportunity only knocks once," as well as Jason's age work against him. Besides, his dad had sex before he married, and he and his mom seem to do all right. So Jason has a choice to make—what shall he choose?

○1. Jason knows his father expects him to have sex, and his teammates admiringly call him a "stud." Frankly, he loves his reputation—until Charlotte, a sometimes date, announces she is pregnant.
GO TO PAGE 128 AND LOOK FOR ○1

○2. Several of Jason's teammates get hold of some pornographic materials and give him a few of the magazines to keep. Jason takes them home and keeps them hidden in his room to look at whenever he feels the urge.
GO TO PAGE 142 AND LOOK FOR ○2

✳✳2 MICHELLE (cont. from page 135)
   A few years later. . .
   "Hurry, kids, the lady from Bethlehem House is here." Michelle was frantically stuffing the last of her personal items into the shopping bag. She and her three kids had been hiding out with friends for four days. They had fled their home, grabbing what little they could, after Jim had stormed out of the house. They didn't want to be there when he returned.
   "Hi, Michelle." Sister Clara's kind face reflected her personality.
   "Say hi to Sister Clara, kids." Michelle scooted the children along and helped them struggle into the van. Each of them carried a bag of clothes and clung to some precious belonging—a teddy bear, doll, or tattered blanket—that could not be left behind. Once the children were secured, Michelle nervously sat next to Sister Clara in the front seat.

For a while they rode along without speaking. Then Sister Clara broke the silence. "I understand there has been violence before," she said sympathetically. "Why did you decide to leave this time?"

"This was different. Jim has shoved and kicked *me* almost since we married, but this was the first time he ever hit one of the kids. I may deserve it, but I know they don't." Michelle glanced back at her children who sat motionless as if in a trance.

Sister Clara pulled the van onto the freeway for the hour's ride to the shelter. "Why do you think you might deserve such treatment?" she asked.

Michelle let out a big sigh. For the first time in days she began to relax. "I've had a lot of men. Jim knows he has to keep control of me. I guess I deserve it."

"Michelle, no one *deserves* to be beaten." Sister Clara checked her rear mirror and moved to the fast lane. "When did you start feeling bad about yourself?"

Michelle shot a glance at the sister and then looked straight forward. "Why do you think I feel bad about myself? Who told you that?"

"A person who marries someone who abuses her and thinks she deserves it can't feel good about herself!"

Michelle laughed unhappily. *I guess it's obvious,* she thought. "Well, a long time ago, I thought I was in control of the relationships I had, but as time went on, I began to realize those guys in high school were right—I was a nothing and a nobody they could do anything with. Jim came along and part of me said, *You can't do any better. At least he's willing to marry you.* And another part said, *He'll keep you in line.*"

"You don't think you can keep yourself in line?"

"I guess I didn't."

Playing games with sex had proven to be an expensive lesson for Michelle involving great losses: peace, safety, self respect, and a healthy marital relationship. In the end, it wasn't her "conquests" who paid, after all.

IF YOU WANT TO EXPLORE OTHER CHOICES
MICHELLE COULD HAVE MADE, RETURN TO
PAGE 16 OR 83.

PORNOGRAPHY: WHAT HARM COULD IT POSSIBLY DO?

Here's what's happening:

O2 JASON: The things Jason sees depicted in the pornographic magazines really turn him on. He finds himself spending more and more time looking at "skin" pictures, reading porno novels, and fantasizing about himself being involved. Then he begins acting out these fantasies with the girls he dates.

Jason's heading for trouble. Let's talk about why, and then continue his story.

Pornography: What harm could it possibly do?

Recently, a teenage boy appeared on a national television show. Why the notoriety? He had become infamous because he had made eighty thousand dollars worth of phone calls to a "dial-a-porn" telephone line. The host and audience clearly thought his act reckless but cute—sort of a "boys will be boys" kind of thing.

As a therapist who deals with many issues of sexuality, I was appalled. The boy was surely addicted to pornography, and the damage to his life would go far beyond the huge financial debt that brought him national attention.

Many others besides the phone company profit immensely from the business of feeding people's misplaced desires. These "services" devastate both those in the "industry" and those who become victims of the product.

Take little Lauren, a preschooler, for instance. Her mother paid for work around the house by allowing the workmen to rape her. When Lauren protested and wanted to run away from the madness of her home, her mother arranged for men to come and take demeaning pictures of her in provocative poses with animals or while the men raped her.

In every case, Lauren's attempts to reach out for help were ignored. She was trapped in a world that humiliated, abused, drugged, and terrorized her. By the time she was finally able to leave that world, she had witnessed the making of snuff films, participated in lewd acts that only the most debauched could dream up, and ultimately had her newborn babies snatched away to be tortured and sacrificed in Satanic rituals.

Lauren's story is not a figment of an overactive imagination. Lauren's story is real. (For Lauren Stratford's story, read *Satan's Underground*, published by Harvest House Publishers; it's the firsthand story of a women caught in the web of pornography.) She is one of thousands who are literal slaves in the hands of powerful businessmen whose line of work happens to be pornography. *Playboy*'s finely coifed women are the tip of a gigantic iceberg whose hidden mass conceals the worst the human mind can conceive. Like Lauren, the majority of the pornographer's subjects don't receive mink coats or stays at the Playboy mansion.

Pornography, whether high class or underworld, demeans human beings. It takes what is meant to be beautiful, complex, and relational and reduces it to its lowest common denominator—a sex-object. It cheapens human life. This is not only true for the Laurens. It is also true for the viewers.

Some people feel that involvement with pornography is a harmless way to become quickly aroused. Pornographic material is often viewed by couples who find it a bypass to heightened sex. It works. And it's easier than working on nurturing your spouse, taking the time to iron out grievances, or becoming a trustworthy person your partner can respond to.

The individual user finds this fantasy outlet safer than a real relationship. "There she is folks, all yours, always available, and never critical."

For reasons we do not understand some people find the world of pornography something they can't just take or leave. They hunger for raunchier, more demeaning, more shocking revelations. Their natural shame forces them to hide their increasing appetite, and this alienates them from satisfying relationships—the very purpose of sex.

Pornography addiction can begin simply enough. For someone who gets turned on by pictures of a lot of skin, maybe the swimsuit issue of *Sports Illustrated* will work fine. But chances are he will crave more and more, and as the material gets worse, his conscience shrivels. If a spouse or someone else comments on the vileness of the material, he dismisses their concerns as prudish. "Everyone looks at this stuff," he rationalizes. Finally, bored by passive involvement, some individuals can't control the urge to act out what they have seen.

To break the cycle of addiction, the treatment is patterned after the twelve-step program of Alcoholics Anonymous. Unfortunately, many people do not get help until they have broken the law. Along the way they have destroyed their marriages, alienated their children, and brought shame and humiliation to others and themselves.

Pornography is "any material depicting sexual activity which, by design and emphasis, encourages and promotes the desire in the observer to engage in illicit sexual activity." (Definition taken from *Human Sexuality in the Christian Life*, published in Newton, Kansas, by the General Conference Mennonite Church in the U.S., in 1988; p. 138.) This relates to the intent of the producer and the effect on the viewer. It is not simply nudity or eroticism. Much of what we see in advertising, the media, and books and magazines is therefore pornographic because of its intent.

144

When someone asks you, *What harm does a little "skin" do?* tell them that first it perverts the meaning of sex. God's plan for sexuality gives meaning to our physical desire, to two sexes, to love, reproduction, and the relationship between a husband and wife. Are we here on earth just to follow our physical drives? Or do we find fulfillment by living up to our Creator's desires for us?

Second, it is harmful because pornography destroys the self-image of women. No one can match the airbrushed beauty of the centerfold model. It is impossible to carry out the many responsibilities of life—work, keeping up household chores, raising children, and so on—and look sensuous all the time. That's not reality. It's an imaginary standard. When her husband chooses pornography, maybe even instead of her, she really feels demeaned, worthless, and rejected.

Third, we need to reject pornography for no other reason than to put an end to the dehumanizing experiences of people like Lauren. People who pay money to feed their ravenous, depraved appetites support financial empires that stagger the imagination. Do you really want to add one penny to their bank accounts?

Finally, is it worth the risk of becoming a victim of your own or someone else's obsession?

What happens next?

O2 JASON (cont. from page 142)

Jason parked in a quiet spot just out of town, a place he and his dates had often come to before. Then he led Jan to a small grove hidden from the road and spread out two blankets. Their kissing and petting quickly led to more. "Aw, come on, Jan. It's not like you don't know what's happening or something. Just give it a try," Jason said in his most persuasive tone.

"What's wrong with just plain ol' sex? We've always had a good time before." Jan wasn't buying it; she began buttoning her blouse.

"I'm bored. I didn't know you were a prude."

"I'm not a prude, but what you're asking me to do is kinky!"

"Kinky can be fun, Jan. Come on," he insisted. "Let's have some fun." In a flash he was on top of her, pulling at her jeans.

"Stop it!" she yelled as she pushed him off her. "You're sick!"

Jason burned. He had had enough of these high school teases. "And you're a whore!" he shouted. "And not even a good one!" He jumped up, grabbed the blankets, and threw them in his truck. Starting the engine, he slammed his foot down on the gas pedal almost before Jan could get in.

As he pulled up in front of her house, Jan jumped out and slammed the door. "Don't ever ask me out again!" she screamed, running up the front walk.

"No chance of that, Baby!" Jason replied sarcastically. *What a dork*, he thought. Imagine getting a conscience now after all they had done. He had simply outgrown her, he decided. Since discovering the world of pornography, he had become more creative in his ideas for sex. Some girls had been willing to go along, but occasionally they freaked out like Jan had tonight.

He was ready for some real action with women who knew what a guy needed. He knew where to find them.

"Hi, sugar, you looking for a good time?" the leggy blond asked, leaning in the car window.

"Sure thing," he replied.

GO TO PAGE 209 AND LOOK FOR ◯2

IT SHOULDN'T HURT
TO BE A KID

Here's what's happening:

■ MICHELLE: Michelle is typical of many girls who have been sexually abused, in that sexuality is the only way she knows to relate to men. Where is that likely to lead her? Will she remain a victim or become a survivor?

Let's examine her options, and then we'll continue her story.

It Shouldn't Hurt to Be a Kid

"Child abuse is legally defined as any act of omission or commission that endangers or impairs a child's physical or emotional health and development," according to the U.S. Attorney General's office.

Frequently, child abuse victims do not receive the help they need. Either no one believes them, or they are accused of "asking for it."

Many victims are threatened into secrecy. Some believe that this is just the way life is. Older children know that if they demand protection, the family will likely break up. Still others, in self-protection, deny its significance or fear losing the only time anyone shows them attention and affection.

A recent survey in a leading medical journal reported that about one out of every four women are sexually abused before they are eighteen. Boys are abused at about half that rate. In the majority of cases, sexual abuse occurs between family members. It is not uncommon for siblings to be involved with one another sexually. In most cases their behavior is simply normal exploration and curiosity. If there is several years' difference in age or if there is coercion, manipulation, or fear involved—if anything is done against the will of one of the children—then it is no longer play but abuse.

Although rape, oral sex, and sodomy (anal intercourse) do occur, sexual abuse quite often involves fondling the genitals, masturbation, and intercourse between the thighs. One-time attacks do happen, but most sexual activity occurs over a long period. Girls are most vulnerable between the ages of 5 and 14; the highest incidence is found at age 11. The most common victim is a middle-class teenager in a second family formed after divorce. Statistically, older teens are at greater risk for serious injuries than younger children because they are capable of some resistance.

Boys are often seduced by older girls or women. Our society suggests that this is merely a rite of passage, but such experiences can be traumatic and leave scars that the victim may or may not connect to the abuse.

Symptoms of abuse in children may include withdrawing, being fearful—especially of specific persons or situations, personality changes, bed wetting, changes in sleep patterns, crying for no apparent reason, clinging, loss of appetite, refusal to go to school, running away, and acting or talking about sex in inappropriate ways for their age.

Teenage victims frequently become promiscuous, run away from home, rebel against all authority, get involved with the wrong crowd and alcohol or other drugs. Research shows that, by far, most teenage girls in trouble with the law have a history of molestation.

Society is showing more concern for abuse victims now due to the discovery that adult behavior is affected by molestation that occurred years before, even when those incidents are blocked from memory. Adult victims of child abuse often suffer from bouts of depression, carry considerable anger, experience a great deal of fear/anxiety, guilt/shame, have difficulty establishing relationships, shut down their feelings, and become subject to repeated victimizations (sexually, at work, in marriage). Many have low self-esteem and sexual problems in marriage.

Much *addictive* behavior can be related to abuse. In addition to substance addiction, a person can become addicted to things like sex and food. People may overeat, for example, to comfort themselves in their pain or to make themselves unattractive so that no one will want them sexually.

People who abuse others have often been abused themselves. Treatment can stop a cycle that results in the sins of the fathers being passed on to the children. (See Ex. 34:7.) When victims becomes free and healthy, they can relate better to others and to God instead of letting past hurts determine their behavior.

There is no way to break the cycle without facing the truth. It is Satan who loves the darkness; the Lord wants us to bring our problems into the light. In doing that, the victim establishes responsibility.

A child is never at fault, no matter how willingly he or she may have participated. Many times there are people who should have stopped what was happening but didn't. Others created an atmosphere that made a child a victim. Parents contribute to abuse when they don't teach their children about sex.

As healing occurs, it is often necessary to confront the people who have abused or contributed to the abuse by their messages or inaction. There is no guarantee that the outcome will result in a lot of warm fuzzies. Confrontations should not be knock-down-drag-out fights. If all parties are open to confrontation, significant family healing can result.

It is often difficult to forgive those who have caused us pain. And when the pain has resulted in failed marriages, substance abuse, and self-defeating behavior, forgiveness may take time. But it is part of becoming whole again. Forgiving should not be confused with trusting a person who has proved untrustworthy.

Moving from *victim* to *survivor* of abuse is a process. It doesn't happen overnight but is helped along by a good counselor and a support group. Most cities have support groups for people who have been abused. Many churches make referrals to counselors experienced in this area.

The task of recovery seems enormous—and perhaps it is—on the human level. But we have a God who can perform miracles. He can and does restore victims of abuse to full, healthy, functional lives, for he is the Mighty Counselor.

What happens next?

■ MICHELLE (cont. from page 147)
Because Michelle has never dealt with the fact that she is a victim of abuse, most of her important decisions reflect the fact that her father took advantage of his position of authority, violated her trust, and undermined her self-image. How do you think Michelle tried to work out her pain?

■1. Like many abused females, Michelle marries before she finishes high school. She and her new husband have many arguments over their sex life.
GO TO PAGE 151 AND LOOK FOR ■1

■2. Michelle becomes very distrustful of men and has a difficult time establishing quality relationships.
GO TO PAGE 185 AND LOOK FOR ■2

SEX IS AS NATURAL AS FALLING OFF A LOG, ISN'T IT?

Here's what's happening:

1 MICHELLE: Michelle can't separate her sexual relationship with her husband from her fear of being out of control and overpowered. No matter how patient her husband is or what he tries, she can't enjoy their lovemaking. After a while, he concludes that he is a terrible lover. Michelle, too, suspects that that is true. After all, men are supposed to satisfy their wives. She begins to notice other things she dislikes about him as well.

Can this marriage last? Let's talk about sex in marriage, and then we'll continue Michelle's story.

Sex Is as Natural as Falling off a Log, Isn't It?

Did you know that even kings can have sexual problems? Song of Solomon, chapter five, tells the sad tale of a king who liked late-night sex and his bride who liked her sleep!

151

Sexual problems can wreck marital happiness. Although some couples hang onto their marriages despite their D-minus performance, most people seem to need an adequate sex life to feel good about the marriage. Studies tell us that the better the sex life, the more likely the couple will describe their marriage as satisfying.

People desire intimacy on many levels, including the sexual. We were made that way. In fact, Scripture implies that married couples should have regular sexual relations. If they decide not to, it should be by mutual agreement, for a limited time, and in order that they might pray! (1 Cor. 7:4–5).

Because it's so hard to avoid sexual involvement when we are single, it's often difficult to imagine any problem with sex when sanctioned by marriage. But God is a realist. He created sex, so he knows that it is not "as simple as falling off a log." That's why he includes a sexual problem in the Bible.

Good sex depends on a lot of factors. Perhaps one of the most important is knowledge. It's hard to be an expert when you don't have a clue what's going on. Sex education consisting solely of information about birth-control methods and how a baby is born won't help sustain a satisfying level of sexual intimacy. The importance of communication, dependency, trust, and the different ways men and women approach sex, aren't usually included in a school curriculum and are rarely discussed in the home or church.

Many people are never told anything about their genitalia or other intricacies of God's design of the body. They often don't even know the proper names. Communicating with their spouse is reduced to trying to break a code:

"Darling, I love it when you touch my 'whatsit.'"

"I know, sweetheart. I feel the same when you stroke my 'weewee.'"

Normal anatomy and physiological responses are frequently mistaken as abnormal, and people develop fears or misconceptions about how things are supposed to be.

Fear that things are not as they should be or the normal size or shape can cause much anxiety. Fear of pain or harm can also cause the body to tense, resulting in the very pain that is dreaded.

152

Fear of poor performance, losing identity, or being deserted, can all affect sexual functioning.

Being raised in a family that was not comfortable with touch affects the sex life. Your upbringing, including what you observed as well as what was said or not said, plays a large part in a person's attitude toward the sexual relationship. Many Christian parents focus on sexual sin and don't get around to presenting sex as a positive gift from God. Sexual feelings are labeled bad and dangerous and we avoid them rather than acknowledge and master them.

The body is unable to register two sensations at once. If it's tense with stress or burning with anger, it can't feel erotic sensations. Modern society provides plenty of both. Poor relationships, demanding jobs, and money worries leave a married spouse with little energy or enthusiasm for sex. Fatigue also takes its toll.

Creatures of habit, we find ourselves stuck in routines that result in boredom. *Oh, its Saturday night. We've eaten, watched TV, and visited the bathroom. Let's see, what else was on the old calendar for today? Ah! Sex! I almost forgot. As soon as the 11 p.m. news is over, I'll go spray on my "Stud" cologne and she'll know it's time.* Ruts kill sexual passion because they reduce sex to a perfunctory performance devoid of spontaneity, symbolism, and sensual awareness.

For most people depression and illness also reduce the desire for sex. Anything that affects natural body functions (sleep, eating, urination, etc.) can affect sex as well.

Both what we learn and the normal circumstances of life affect the way we adjust to marital sexuality. Without awareness and appropriate intervention, difficulties tend to escalate and secondary problems begin. Memories of abuse may send a message that says "I'm a rotten person" or "Who am I to have a good sex life?" or "Every time he touches me there, I remember uncle Charlie and what he did."

Talking openly about our needs, disappointments, and pleasures is the most important step in preventing and overcoming problems. When a sexual problem persists, a wise couple would seek the help of a third party. Pastors and counselors familiar with sexual counseling can help couples restore or create a relationship like the model in Song of Solomon.

Television and movies suggest that the best sex is outside of marriage. This is not true. In marriage we find the most sex, the greatest variety, and the most orgasms. Extramarital sex is often less free and enjoyable. The "extras" that make sex good (a committed relationship for life, feelings of security and trust, and freedom to be yourself) are missing outside of marriage.

Now, what about our king with the sexual problem? The biblical solution would please the best modern-day sex therapist. King Solomon does not belittle his wife for her selfishness and tendency to take him for granted. He doesn't ignore her or threaten to turn elsewhere. He simply tells her how much he still cares, leaves her a gift, and promises her a much-longed-for trip to the country.

She rethinks her response, allows herself to think erotically of him, makes herself available, and lets him know her intentions by a sensuous dance performed just for him. The king knew she needed romance and he provided it. She knew what he found attractive and made an effort to meet his needs. Each took responsibility for the part of the problem he or she had control over. Both changed their behavior to meet the partner's needs.

Men and women approach sex differently. Men respond more to the visual and physical while women focus on romance, the setting, and how the relationship is going.

Song of Solomon gives us a realistic picture of sex in marriage. Despite problems that can occur, it is filled with joy, passion, and pleasure. If our marital sex falls short (and it will because this is a fallen world), we can still maximize what we can have. To do less is to sit around in a wading pool when we have a whole ocean to enjoy!

What happens next?

■1 MICHELLE (cont. from page 151)

Michelle squeezed her nervous husband's hand as she and Howard stepped into the consultation room.

Mrs. Thomas, a Christian therapist in her early fifties, closed the door and took a seat in one of the three overstuffed chairs in the room. "Michelle, you have made real progress," she said, motioning for them to be seated. "I'm so pleased you and your husband are here together so we can begin establishing a new sexual relationship for the two of you."

Michelle smiled. "It's been a long journey!"

"The turning point really came when you chose to speak about the incest in your family," Mrs. Thomas reminded her. "Satan loves the dark. As long as we keep our hurts and pains hidden, he is able to keep us in turmoil." She turned and spoke directly to Howard. "Your wife and I have spent many hours in prayer, reliving some very painful times from her past. We brought them into the light so that Christ could come in and heal."

Howard began to relax. "I know it's been tough, but I can see such a difference already. We talk so much more," his voice was tinged with excitement.

Michelle had begun to see her husband with new eyes in recent weeks. He cared about her needs before his own. She loved him for that. How had she missed it before? Her eyes filled with tears as she spoke. "Your patience once I began my sessions with Mrs. Thomas really helped, Howard. Thank you." She looked up. "And my group—my group helped too. It's good to know you're not the only one this happens to."

"Insight, forgiveness, and experiencing God's love and protection contribute to the healing process, but that's not all that needs to be done," Mrs. Thomas replied. "You know how your marriage got in the jam it did. Now we need to do some specific things that will help you enjoy your sexual relationship."

The therapist's controlled voice made Michelle feel confident. She reached over and took Howard's hand again. Howard gave it a little squeeze.

Michelle hadn't felt this hopeful for years. A big smile brightened her face.

Mrs. Thomas saw Michelle and Howard for eight more sessions. They literally began their sexual relationship anew by following classic sexual therapy techniques. There were tough times, but they dealt with the real issues openly. Before, they didn't know the source of the problem. Now true healing could take place because both were willing to make the effort, and their chief therapist was The Great Physician.

GO TO PAGE 101 AND LOOK FOR ■1

156

SO YOU THINK YOU KNOW HOW TO TALK

Here's what's happening:

■2 MICHELLE: Michelle decides to put her dating life on hold temporarily. She accepts the fact that although she has learned a lot, she still has a long way to go. Relationships based on more than sex are complex and challenging. Her goal is to learn to create intimacy through communication.

How do you do that? Let's look at the ways, and then we'll continue Michelle's story.

So You Think You Know How to Talk

Have you ever read a court transcript? The words are all there, but they hardly make sense. Missing are the raised eyebrow, the threatening look, the disdainful saunter away from the stand. Our words are only half of what we say.

As a psychologist, I need to look carefully for discrepancies between what my clients' words tell me and what his or her body language reveals. Add age differences (Is *gnarly* good or bad, anyway?), cultural differences (Many cultures find it rude to look you directly in the eye while Americans are suspicious of anyone who doesn't), sex differences, and so on, and it is a wonder we communicate at all!

Communication is particularly bad between parents and teens. Teenagers are fearful that they will either be misunderstood or be given advice. Teenagers are pretty smart.

Communication is often poorest when it comes to sex. Kids are afraid any questions they ask will be incriminating, and adults have never spoken openly or used "those words" in public. Accommodating sons and daughters may pretend not to need any information just to spare parents the pain.

All this creates major problems in marriage. Having never seen or practiced healthy open dialogue, husbands and wives don't know how to communicate their sexual needs. For example:

He: "I just don't know what else to do. I've read all the books. I try all kinds of great techniques. I've memorized the ten most erotic spots on women. What more can I do?"
She: "Try flowers."

We rarely get what we want unless we clearly tell someone what we want. Sexual communication is hampered by the belief that men should know all there is about making women happy—the old "If he really loved me, he would know how to make me respond" myth. Many women feel it's inappropriate for them to spell out their sexual needs—the old "Nice girls don't have those needs" myth.

Research tells us that husbands and wives who view their sex life as sexually satisfying are almost always good communicators. This does not mean they sit around over coffee and share what turns them on although there is nothing wrong with that. It does mean that they are able to share sometimes in a nonverbal way, what they need in order to be responsive. Often, it has nothing to do with sexual techniques but involves feeling loved, being valued, and being listened to.

Take responsibility for good communication in a relationship. Speak for yourself. Compare scene one with scene two below:

Scene 1

She: "Let's do something."

He: "What do you want to do?"

She: "Oh, I don't care." *(But I hope you want to go to the zoo, 'cause I do).*

He: *(Maybe she wants to go to the mall.)* "Let's go to the mall." *(But I sure would like to go to the zoo.)*

She: *(How boring! He has no imagination. But if that's where he wants to go. . .)* "Great, let's do it."

Scene 2

She: "I feel like doing something today."

He: "Got anything in mind?"

She: "I would love to go to the zoo."

He: "So would I."

In the first scene neither got what they wanted. They were fearful that putting their desires on the line might bring up differences and cause a fight. In the second scene each clearly knew how the other felt, so each could risk being honest.

But what if you don't want the same thing? The people we like are not our archenemies. They want to get along with us. Once each person's desires are in the open—and you don't have to fish to figure them out—two good brains can go to work on the same set of facts. Usually you can find a solution both feel comfortable with. If you can't communicate with a boyfriend about what you would like to do or where you would like to eat, you won't likely be able to communicate in the bedroom after marriage.

Talking about sex is hard because we've rarely seen anyone do it! And because our egos are tied up with how we see ourselves as a sexual person, rejection by someone we love or inability to be responsive shatters our self- concept. We'd rather avoid the problem than confront it.

If you are scared to risk honest communication with people you care about, try the following:

1. Take responsibility by starting your sentences with the word "I." Example: "I'm hungry." "I need you to give me a hug."

2. Avoid beginning sentences with *You* or *Let's* or *We*. Compare:

Scene 1
Guy: "Would you like to go to the show?"
Gal: "I don't know, would you?"
Guy: "Whatever you want is fine with me."
Gal: "I just want you to be happy."

Scene 2
Guy: "I feel like going to a movie tonight."
Gal: "I was hoping we could drop by Jenny's. A lot of the kids are going to be there. Would you mind going to a late movie?"
Guy: "No problem."

3. Forget words like *ought, should,* and *have to,* and substitute *might, could,* and *I want to.* Example: "I should [in other words, she expects it, so I have to] kiss Karen good-night." Compare that with "I could [if my heart is in it and it seems appropriate] kiss Karen good night."

4. Don't use questions to mask what you are really saying. Example: "Why are you mad?" often means "I feel that you're angry with me, and that makes me uncomfortable."

5. Don't use the words *always* and *never.* Try words like *up to now* or *in the past.* Example: "You always get 'lovey-dovey' when I've had a bad day" Compare that with: "Up to now, it seems like you are most affectionate when it's hardest for me to respond."

6. Throw out *I don't know* or *I don't care.* You do care, but you may not feel strongly one way or the other. Be clear about where you stand. Example:

Guy: "What do you want for lunch?"
Gal: "I don't care."
Guy: "Great! How about fried worms?"
Gal: "Maybe I do care after all. How about a hamburger?"

Use your dating relationships to practice good communication techniques. The habits you establish now will help you be wary of

160

people who have a problem with communicating openly and honestly. And when you marry, it will ensure a more peaceful partnership and a more pleasurable sexual relationship.

What happens next?

■2 MICHELLE (cont. from page 157)

A few years later. . .

"Guess what!" Michelle practically danced through her friend's doorway.

"I can't imagine, but I suspect it's made you happy," Mrs. Gardner said with a little laugh. "Sit down. I just made some tea."

Michelle flung herself into the nearest chair—her favorite, the one with the flowers that were starting to wear off the arms. Many times before, that chair had provided comfort and support when she and Mrs. Gardner had confronted issues of her past. Those big arms had held her Bible as the two searched Scripture for God's promise of forgiveness and unconditional love.

"For heaven's sake, tell me." Mrs. Gardner sat the teapot down on the little table between them. Two cups were already in place. *Just like they were waiting for me to visit,* Michelle thought.

In one breath she announced, "Paul has asked me to marry him—and I've said yes—and we're going to pick the rings out Saturday!"

"Oh, how grand!" exclaimed Mrs. Gardner, pouring their tea.

"Back when I couldn't trust myself to date, I never thought this would ever happen." She pulled her feet up into the chair and took a sip of tea before continuing. "And even after I risked dating again, and then blew it those two times—if you and Tom hadn't been around to talk to, I don't know what I would have done."

"I'm glad we could be there. But you did your part, too." Mrs. Gardner never missed an opportunity to encourage. "You confessed your sin, accepted forgiveness, determined not to focus on your failures, and tried again. Learning to walk God's way starts with baby steps."

"The neatest thing is that my relationship with Paul has grown

161

slowly." Michelle almost glowed. "We haven't had sex, and yet I feel closer to him than anyone I've ever known."

Mrs. Gardner took a long drink of her tea. "Are you sure there is no history of abuse in his family?" she asked.

Unwrapping her legs and symbolically planting them firmly on the floor, Michelle responded enthusiastically, "There is none. I even checked with some family members to be sure. That's one of the first things we talked about as our relationship began to deepen. My dad was abused, and he abused me. I want the cycle to stop right there."

And it did. Michelle and Paul spent hours and hours getting to know one another, communicating their history, growth, and needs. The time was well spent. By the time they married, they had already resolved many potentially difficult issues. The marriage was a good one.

IF YOU WOULD LIKE TO EXPLORE OTHER CHOICES MICHELLE COULD HAVE MADE, RETURN TO PAGE 16 OR 150.

GROWING UP SEXY

Here's what's happening:

◯ MICHELLE: Even though Michelle looks like she is ready to tackle adult tasks and responsibilities, her body is still maturing, and her mind is still that of a child. She thinks she knows everything she needs to know, but she has a lot to learn.

We'll continue Michelle's story as soon as we discuss some of what she still doesn't know.

Growing Up Sexy

Remember your seventh grade class? Maybe you're in one now. The girls looked like something out of an old "B" movie, "Amazon Women Conquer Junior High." The guys, on the other hand, more closely resembled "Pee Wee Visits the Lunch Room."

When I taught seventh grade, my smallest student, a boy, weighed 57 pounds. The largest, a girl, tipped the scale at 206.

When it comes to maturing, we need to keep two things in mind: 1. Without any help from us, our bodies mature and prepare for reproduction. 2. They do it on their own time.

Much as we would like to speed up or slow down the process, our input—be it prayers, potions, miracle drugs advertised in the *Enquirer,* or hanging upside down thirty minutes a day—are doomed. Our biological time clock refuses to be tampered with.

For example, you know you are capable of sweeping that dark-haired beauty in your science class off her feet. It's just that, at the moment, you happen to be closer to her feet than her heart. Or, perhaps you still enjoy playing with Barbie and Ken (even though you have to hide in the closet so your younger brother won't spot you), but your 32-C bra turns on a multitude of guys who want to play for real.

Early or late development can heap on grief at an already vulnerable time. It is a good idea to check with your parents to see what family patterns you can expect. Ask your mom how she dealt with being the only one who had nothing to train in a training bra. How did your dad feel about being a 45-pound weakling in the Land of Gonads?

By far the most difficult adjustment for a girl is early development. A child's mind and an adult body thrust her into a world she is simply not able to handle. If you are in this situation, talk it over with your parents, a counselor, or another trustworthy adult. A growth spurt announces, "It's new body time." For males, rapid growth usually occurs somewhere between the ages of 12 1/2 and 16. It may start anywhere between the ages of 10 1/2 and 16 and be completed by 13 1/2 to 17 1/2. Girls grow most rapidly between the ages of 10 1/2 and 14.

Although girls often begin to mature physically a full two years before boys, their menstruation cycle only precedes boys' ejaculation capability by about six months. Ejaculation can occur a year or so after the penis starts to grow. A boy can masturbate and have orgasms before he can ejaculate. Pubic hair can be used as a cue. Ejaculation can occur 3—4 months after the first curly pubic hair appears. Voice changes follow.

Often the most upsetting changes are acne and gynecomastia (breast development in males experienced by 80% of all boys). These are temporary, but zits and breasts can be rough when you've also just spotted the girl of your dreams!

164

A girl will usually have her first period three-fourths through her growth spurt and 2 1/2 years after the first pubic hair. By then her breasts have been around, at least in their beginning stages, for three or four years. Ovulation can occur before menstruation begins, so it is possible for a girl to get pregnant without having had her first period.

Parts Is Parts

A grown man's penis is about the length of a finger, though thicker. When it is stimulated and filled with blood, it may increase slightly in diameter and become about six inches in length. A man whose penis is erect is said to have an erection. Most males know that erections can occur at the oddest times. Young men have them as a result of intense emotion (like when they are cheering for the team), when it is cold, when their clothing has rubbed against them, and when they see a girl they like. An erection can be eliminated by simply ignoring it.

Penis size has nothing to do with satisfying a woman. All penises are approximately the same size when erect though there might be more variation in a nonerect state. Unlike whales and dogs, there are no bones in a human penis. Erection must be the result of the proper mental and physical stimulation.

The most sensitive part of the penis is the tip or *glans*. Some males have a foreskin (a loose sheath of skin) over the glans. Others had it removed through circumcision, usually at birth. Sexually it makes no difference. For health reasons it is important to keep "smegma" (a thick, ill-smelling secretion) from building up under the foreskin. The scrotum, or "balls," contain the testicles, epididymis (the area where sperm matures), and vas deferens (the tubes that carry the sperm). The testes produce new sperm from puberty until death, whereas, in the female, the ovaries at birth contain all the eggs they will ever have.

Sperm are tiny (500 side by side would measure one inch), tadpole-shaped creatures. They are stored in *seminal vesicles* inside the body. Fluid is added by the vesicles and the prostate gland. The mixture of sperm and fluid is known as semen. Several mechanisms work together to keep the sperm healthy: to maintain the perfect temperature the scrotum draws near the body if it is cold and hangs lower if hot. Also because urine and semen both use the urethra to leave the body, a valve ensures that they do not mix, and a secretion passes through to neutralize the acid of the urine. This pre-ejaculate fluid can sometimes contain sperm. That is why withdrawal is such a poor birth control method since the male has no sensation when this preliminary fluid will be released.

The sensation of orgasm occurs when the muscles of the prostate and others near it contract, propelling the semen down the urethra (the tube from the bladder to the end of the penis).

Though males use the same organs for reproduction, pleasure, and urination, females have specific structures for each function. The *clitoris*, highly sensitive like the glans, has no other purpose except pleasure. Yet in our society girls rarely learn anything about this part of their bodies.

Ovaries house approximately 400,000 immature eggs (200 side by side would measure one inch). Only a small portion of them mature and are released. Sometimes females are aware of a mid-cycle pain that signals the release of the egg. Since the sensation may occur before, during, or after ovulation, it is not reliable for birth control. Waving thread-like appendages of the Fallopian tube lure the egg inside the tube, where it spends about three days. This is where fertilization is likely to occur.

In anticipation of a fertilized egg entering the uterus (the womb), the endometrium (the uterus lining) becomes thick and rich in blood vessels. If there is no fertilized egg, it sluffs off at regular intervals. The sluffing of blood and tissue is called menstruation. A woman may or may not be affected by the hormonal changes of this time. The important thing is for her to be aware of her pattern and make the appropriate adjustments.

The uterus itself is a pear-shaped organ about three inches long. It is remarkable in its strength and stretchability. Its lower portion is called the cervix and is located at the top of the vagina. The vagina is an organ used in reproduction, it is the birth canal, it is the place sperm is deposited, and it is also a site of sexual pleasure.

The lower one-third of the vagina is very sensitive. It and the clitoris provide the most sexual pleasure. Orgasm occurs when these areas, swollen with blood, contract in a rhythmic fashion.

Sexy for a Lifetime

All these changes are rather dramatic, but they are merely activating a system that has been in limited operation since birth. It's like putting gas into a car that hasn't been driven for twelve or thirteen years. At first it may be jerky and bumpy to operate, but after a while it's gliding down the highway. Puberty enables the body to do what it was designed to do—reproduce.

It is not, however, the time when the sexual response system begins to work. That has been in operation since birth. At least half of all boy babies will have their first erection before they leave the delivery room, and girl babies' vaginas will lubricate within a few hours. Each of us has been born with the ability to experience erotic feelings. Our attitude about our sexuality is very much related to those who cared for us.

If we were handled gently and the pleasure we found in our bodies was affirmed, we will likely grow up thankful for a body that can feel and respond. If we were denied pleasure from our bodies, we will likely grow up filled with shame and embarrassment. If we never saw our parents enjoying a healthy interaction as men and women, we don't get a message about sex as a bond and unifier. Before kindergarten, we learn our most crucial lessons of sex education—our gender, what sex means between men and women, and our body as a source of sexual pleasure.

One major difference between men and women is that men cannot reproduce without sexual pleasure, but women can. A woman's reproductive system works automatically, but her sexual response system is under both her conscious and unconscious control.

The primary areas of sexual pleasure for a female are the internal and external lips of the vulva, the muscular tissue surrounding the vagina, the lower portion of the vagina, and the clitoris. Secondarily are the mouth, lips, breasts, skin, and anus. Different women perceive pleasure from each of these areas on a scale uniquely theirs. The emphasis they give an area can change with age, experience, and different times.

Men find their sexual response far less dependent on externals, and there is less variation between them than women. Most men find intercourse the most satisfying sexual act. Women often are more responsive to stimulation with a finger, mouth, or other techniques yet prefer intercourse because of the symbolic meaning it holds for them.

Both men and women go through four stages of sexual response.

1. *Excitement.* The first sign of arousal in males is erection. In females it is lubrication that comes through the vaginal walls.
2. *Plateau.* This stage may be short or long. As blood enters the genital areas, there is pleasurable swelling and general body involvement. Most intercourse takes place in this stage.
3. *Orgasm.* Orgasm takes less than six to fifteen seconds and results from a series of muscular contractions. Some women are able to have more than one orgasm. Capacity for orgasm varies greatly among women.
4. *Resolution.* Everything (respiration, heartbeat, blood flow, muscle contractions) begins to return to normal. Men require a period of time, the *refractory* period, before they can become aroused again. How long depends on the individual and his age.

Conclusion

When I was a little girl, I thought sperm floated through the air. I lived in terror that I might become impregnated by getting on an elevator filled with strange men! I doubt if your fears are so far-fetched! It is important to get correct information. Go to responsible experts and check out your concerns. Read books, ask questions, and most importantly understand that it is healthy to feel good about your body. If you don't, analyze the messages about sex in your home. If they don't line up with sex as a gift from God, you are a victim of misinformation.

What happens next?

○ MICHELLE (cont. from page 163)
Michelle's home situation is so bad that the most important thing on her mind is getting out. She dreams about a family of her own and making a place that is filled with love. Sex will be beautiful, and there will be no need to fear. Is she being realistic? What's she likely to find instead? Make a choice:

○1. Michelle is pregnant when she marries. Her husband complains about feeling trapped and spends a lot of time with his former friends. At first, she is so preoccupied with the baby that she doesn't mind. But after a while, she too, begins to feel confined and lonely. She wishes her life could change.
GO TO PAGE 108 AND LOOK FOR ○1

○2. Michelle and her husband use a variety of birth control methods. It is hard because Michelle has irregular periods. She gets pregnant within the first six months. She and her husband feel they cannot afford a baby.
GO TO PAGE 128 AND LOOK FOR ○2

HOMOSEXUALITY

Here's what's happening:

■ ERIC: Eric becomes increasingly aware of how different he is from his friends. They seem totally taken with girls—the way they look, the way they smell. His friends fight over girls, while Eric couldn't care less. He reads an article in a news magazine about homosexuality. *That must be it*, he decides. *I am a homosexual*.

○2 ERIC: Eric sincerely wants to obey God. He prays earnestly for wisdom and discernment. Much of the time, however, he needs strength and power to overcome the real, driving attraction he feels for other males.

What is homosexuality? Let's examine that questions and then continue Eric's story.

Homosexuality

It is easier to define homosexual behavior than it is to define a homosexual. Homosexual behavior involves sexual intimacy with someone of the same sex. Taking into account the physical limitations, two men or two women do virtually the same things a man and woman do. Homosexual experiences do not *make* a person a homosexual. Neither do occasional same-sex fantasies or "crushes."

Sometimes, usually with help, the person can discover the origin of his or her homosexual behavior. Commonly, sexual and physical abuse are contributing factors. Homosexual behavior, in some instances, has been learned and reinforced as the only place a person feels loved, appreciated, or powerful. For many, there are a number of contributory factors that, added together, reinforce the idea that a person's orientation is for the same sex. Occasionally, the cause appears to be a mystery.

A person can be reoriented to a heterosexual lifestyle instantaneously through God's supernatural intervention, but more frequently it is a long, slow task. For some, victory means no longer engaging in homosexual behavior but living with the knowledge that homosexual desires might be with them the rest of their lives. It is similar to the way an alcoholic must accept his life-long vulnerability to alcohol. Others can become reoriented slowly, and they are eventually able to establish healthy marriages.

People who label themselves homosexuals yield to a lifestyle that is not God's plan. First Corinthians 6:9—10 mentions homosexuality in a list of behavior that is not pleasing to God. Then verse eleven says, "That is what some of you were. But you were washed, you were sanctified, you were justified in the name of the Lord Jesus Christ." Homosexuals do not have to remain trapped in a lifestyle of sin any more than anyone else. Christ promises freedom and forgiveness.

Scripture clearly teaches that men or women who participate in a sexual relationship with the same sex deny the order God created. It is sin (Rom. 1:24—25). God designed two sexes for a purpose. Each brings unique aspects of his or her sex to the relationship. And in the union of their social, psychological, and sexual relationship, two miraculously become one. In the beginning God declared that alone, man was "not good." Only after woman was brought to man was humankind declared "very good."

171

Together, man and woman mirror the image of God. This is never possible in a same-sex relationship.

There are those in our society who say you can't change an "alternate lifestyle" or sexual preference. Verse 32 of Romans 1 speaks of them: "Although they know God's righteous decree that those who do such things deserve death, they not only continue to do these very things but also approve of those who practice them." Of course practicing homosexuals who feel trapped in their lifestyle do not want others to realize there is a way out. Convinced that they cannot change, their self-esteem demands that they fight for acceptance and status through gay-rights organizations.

Some seek to justify homosexual behavior through reinterpretation of Scripture. Romans 1:26–27 speaks of exchanging natural functions for the unnatural and some argue that if you are "naturally" born homosexual the unnatural thing would be to be heterosexual. But no one has proven that homosexuality is a natural orientation.

Others declare that since we no longer live under the law, the law of love (including homosexual love) reigns. It is not true, however, that God no longer has any laws for his people.

The New Testament gives us the law of Christ. Many commands are new, but some are not. For example, we no longer stone people or refuse to eat dairy foods and meat together. But Old Testament commands concerning rape, murder, stealing, and homosexuality are repeated in the New Testament. They were sins under the law, and they continue to be sins under grace. Leviticus 18:22, and 20:13 are strong passages against homosexual behavior, and they are still relevant today.

Homosexuals can hold onto God's promise that victory, as the individual and the Lord define it, is possible. "Thanks be to God that, though you used to be slaves to sin, you wholeheartedly obeyed the form of teaching to which you were entrusted. You have been set free from sin and have become slaves to righteousness" (Rom. 6:17–18).

If you have difficulty relating to someone who prefers a same-sex relationship, remember that Jesus always made a distinction between the sin and the sinner. Jesus said he came to heal the sick because the well had no need of his ministry (Matt. 9:12). Our ostracism of the homosexual bears little resemblance to his ministry. Christian fellowship is an important part of the homosexual's journey to wellness.

What happens next?

■ ERIC (cont. from page 170)
Eric is really suffering. He needs information, but it isn't readily available. He is afraid to bring the matter up because that would be the same as admitting it was true. Since other guys around his age were hot for girls and he wasn't, homosexuality seemed the only other alternative. Do you think Eric is gay because his experience seems different from other guys his age? How can he find out? Make a choice:

■1. Eric sees an ad for a gay-rights group that meets at a local university campus. He decides to investigate.
GO TO PAGE 175 AND LOOK FOR ■1

■2. Eric hears about a place where gays are supposed to hang out. He is afraid to go. But tired of feeling different and not fitting in, he gathers up the courage and visits.
GO TO PAGE 19 AND LOOK FOR ■2

O2 ERIC (cont. from page 170)
As soon as Eric got home he headed for the phone. Without even taking off his coat, he grabbed the phone and dialed. "Hi, Cam," He heard the tremor in his own voice. His encounter with Mrs. Murphy had left him shaken and upset.

"You sound upset. What's up?" Cam was perceptive as usual.

Eric's hands trembled. "A lady at church just gave me her two bits about how I would be healed if my spiritual life was in order— that I obviously had unconfessed sin in my life," he said.

"Oh, yes, I know those well-meaning types," his friend replied. "They can shake you to the core, can't they?"

"Cam, I know we've been over this a thousand times, but it

always throws me when someone suggests that my homosexual desires are still with me because my walk with God isn't right."

Eric had met Cam, who was older than Eric, at a support group meeting for homosexual Christian men. Cam became Eric's assigned buddy. As in Alcoholics Anonymous, they were to be accountable to one another.

"Let me ask you something," said Cam. "Are you taking time out daily to have a quiet time with the Lord?"

"Yes," Eric answered. He had discovered that without a regular prayer life, he was far more vulnerable to his desires.

"Are you fellowshiping regularly with Christians who are committed to walking God's way?" Cam continued.

"Yes."

"Are you careful of the movies, videos, and magazines you're viewing?"

"I'm trying," Eric replied. "Sometimes I get a fantasy rolling before I even realize it, but I'm convicted when that happens, and I confess it and ask for the Lord's strength."

"Eric, it's not our place to demand that God change our circumstances. It's our place to be obedient to his Word. You're doing that."

"Sometimes it's tough to know why healing doesn't come when you want it so badly." He sighed. "You know the Lord doesn't want you to act on your homosexual desires."

"Sometimes healing means grace to live with your situation. We have to remember not to look at healing with our human eyes only." Cam paused. "You feeling better?"

"Yeah. Thanks, Cam."

GO TO PAGE 84 AND LOOK FOR ○2

IF IT FEELS GOOD, DO IT

Here's what's happening:

1 ERIC: Eric finds a warm welcome at the gay-rights meeting. During the social time afterward, several of the men tell him that they felt like him before they "came out." Eric becomes more and more convinced that he is gay. One man points out that since so much "gay bashing" goes on, many people like Eric are reluctant to admit what they know in their heart. It feels like this might be true of Eric.

What's likely to happen to Eric if he merely follows his feelings? We'll continue his story as soon as we've examined that question.

If It Feels Good, Do It

"If it feels good, do it!" That was the rallying call of the 70s. People did what they felt like doing, and divorce hit an all-time record high, sexual diseases spread rapidly, women aborted their babies, and drugs robbed good minds of their ability to even judge what felt good! Making life decisions on the basis of "what feels good" has its consequences. But even today, many decide when to get involved sexually by whether or not "it feels good."

175

Sex *is* going to feel good because it was made to feel good. The setting determines the correctness of your sexual decision-making, not the feeling.

Overindulging in ice cream also feels good, but the extra pounds a few days later hardly seem worth it. Overeating at Thanksgiving seems the only tradition-upholding thing to do until the stomachache hits. Speeding on the freeway is exhilarating until the police officer asks if you know how fast you were going.

The length of time it takes to indulge somehow never equals the length of the consequences. Life's like that. We want immediate gratification. Our focus is so blurred by the promise of pleasure that we can't see further than the cherry on the top of an ice cream soda or the orgasm that sends shivers through the body.

On rational days, the thought of exchanging thirty minutes of pleasure for the potential of a lifetime, or even one hour of pain, hardly seems worth it. God didn't give us our feelings to be magical indicators of how to live our lives. Feelings rarely indicate what is wise. They have their own job to do. Communicating feelings creates intimacy and closeness with others. Without them life is as captivating as a black-and-white television program. When a person has thought through a decision, asked God for wisdom, and listened to the guidance of the Holy Spirit, then he or she can allow feelings their rightful place, confident that any consequences will be ones he or she can gladly bear.

What happens next?

1 ERIC (cont. from page 175)

"You nervous, Eric?" John asked.

Eric took a deep breath. He had met John at the first gay-rights meeting he attended. John was a lawyer in his thirties. They had met several times for coffee, and Eric appreciated how patient and understanding John had been.

"No," he lied. Trying to think of something constructive to do with his hands, Eric took an art book from the coffee table and faked fascination.

John came over and sat on the sofa across from him. "I was, my first time," he admitted. Handing Eric a glass of wine, he sat back with one of his own.

Eric closed the book and took a sip of wine. "There has to be a first time, sometime, I guess."

The exact order of events from then on are no longer clear to Eric. Convinced he was homosexual, there was no need to deny the inevitable. John was a nice guy, and Eric had to admit he found him attractive.

GO TO PAGE 96 AND LOOK FOR ∎1

THE CHURCH AND THE HOMOSEXUAL

Here's what's happening:

■2 ERIC: Eric recognizes that much of the love he feels for Bill is *eros*. But he does care about and enjoy Bill for himself. Neither are comfortable with the promiscuous lifestyle they see among many gays, so they commit to a life-long partnership. This does not bring more acceptance as they had hoped. Their efforts to join a local church meet with ridicule, ostracism, and condemnation.

○1 ERIC: Eric sees the conflict between his faith and his sexual orientation. He is right to ask God for the solution. God can heal instantly. He has healed many homosexuals that way. But more frequently, he heals over a period of time. It is a process. God's way of doing things is not always ours. Sometimes he wants to deal with other issues first.

Let's examine the conflict Eric finds himself in, and then we'll continue his story.

The Church and the Homosexual

The Christian community has been uncomfortable dealing with issues of homosexuality. The tendency is to push gays out of fellowship, thinking "out of sight, out of mind." It's easy to bunch all homosexuals together as faceless perverts who spend all their time thinking of ways to infect heterosexuals with AIDS. But you stop thinking that way when you discover one of those faceless perverts is your brother, son, daughter, or long-time friend.

Barbara Johnson, mother of a homosexual son, began a ministry for parents of homosexuals called Spatula Ministries. The name reflects her initial reaction (and the reaction of most Christian parents) upon learning the homosexual orientation of the child they raised, loved, and cared for. It is called Spatula Ministries because the shock is so great that "parents have to be scraped off the ceiling."

When there is an accident, illness, or death in the family, Christian friends rally around with support. But when parents discover their child is living a gay lifestyle, no one brings meals to the house or even wants to talk about it. Isolated in their shock and shame, they must endure the pain and questions alone.

The homosexual usually can't comfort or educate the parent, either, since he or she has also accepted many stereotypes as truths. Many gays cut themselves off from the family, immersing themselves in the gay lifestyle. Others go to great lengths to conceal their orientation. Rarely do homosexuals find a church that goes further than conviction, so they quit going.

Christians often feel uncomfortable learning about homosexuality because others may view their interest as suspect. Scriptural commands against it are the source of great controversy. Church tradition has no place for the homosexual Christian.

If scientific research could prove genetically that some individuals are born gay, this would eliminate much of the controversy for some. For others, this is a moot point. One thing that everybody agrees on, however, is that for the most part, the Church's ministry to homosexuals has not reflected Jesus' compassion.

A few churches, with the encouragement of researcher Elizabeth Moberly, Ph.D., are pioneering new programs that enfold homosexuals in a special way instead of driving them out. These programs of healing are based on the observation that human beings develop in stages. As we mature, moving from one plateau to another, we eventually reach the maturity level of Genesis 2:24, leaving our parents and cleaving to an opposite-sex partner.

In order to advance to the next developmental stage, a person's needs and desires of the current stage must be met. Moberly suggests that when something disrupts the attachment to the same sex parent, some people get "stuck" at that stage and seek fulfillment through same-sex relationships. Others in the same situation resolve the issue and go on to develop heterosexual relationships. No one knows what causes the different reactions. The disruption may or may not be caused by the same-sex parent's behavior. It may result from a separation trauma that is long or short, accidental or planned (death, hospitalization, business trip). One child may protest, fall into despair, and then become somewhat detached, going on to the next stage while another develops unhealthy yearnings and a defensive detachment to overcome the deficit.

We all know what it's like to be denied something we are really hungry for. It is not sick for a child to desire a satisfying and secure relationship with a parent. It is not sick to need this same-sex love. The sick part is when the parent does not fulfill that need. The homosexual feels an attraction toward the same sex but also revulsion. His or her ambivalence may lead to promiscuous behavior—the desire to be close but not too close.

God planned for men and women to be interdependent in all areas of their lives. That is what made humankind good. Our gender is defined by loving someone different from ourselves. To be truly heterosexual, a person needs to be different from the person loved. The person loved fulfills our identity, providing a contrast against which we see ourselves clearly.

In order for the homosexual to relate to the opposite sex, the deficit of same-sex love must be filled. This treatment is the exact opposite of what most therapists and the Church have traditionally practiced. Rather than trying to retrain a person to desire the

180

opposite sex, the homosexual must make a concerted effort to find same-sex fellowship and love without a sexual relationship. Then defensive detachments can be undone and unmet needs met. The healing power of love, coupled with healing prayer therapy, is proving helpful in ministering to the homosexual with a problem of developmental issues.

Individuals may engage in homosexual activities because of a variety of psychological processes. Help in exploring the life events, assumptions, and even physiological propensities that have convinced a person of his homosexuality is another important part of getting well. But loving and sensitive therapy can uncover these and provide freedom. Still others may have willfully chosen a lifestyle of sin, which they need to confess.

A model program that has provided hope and practical support for individuals trying to escape a homosexual lifestyle is Desert Stream Ministries, 1415 Santa Monica Mall, Santa Monica, CA 90401—(213) 395-9137. Desert Stream is a member of Exodus International (P.O. Box 2121, San Rafael, CA 94912, 415-454-1017), an international coalition of ministries proclaiming the message of liberation from homosexuality through repentance and faith in Jesus as Savior and Lord.

Neither the Church nor the individual Christian can bring healing to the sick without a ministry of love.

What happens next?

■2 ERIC (cont. from page 178)

As soon as Eric got home, he simultaneously tossed his keys in the key basket and opened the refrigerator. "Hi, Bill," he said, looking for that leftover pizza he thought he remembered seeing there.

Bill knew exactly what Eric was looking for. "It's gone," he called.

"What are you, a mind-reader?" Eric asked.

"After three years with you, I'd have to have parked my brains elsewhere not to know that if there's leftover pizza you'll be looking for it as soon as you come through the door."

Eric laughed. He was a creature of habit. He loved traditions, like the way his family always celebrated Thanksgiving with the gathering of the whole clan. He missed that. He missed a lot of things. He hadn't seen his family in over two years.

"Hey, don't forget. Tonight we promised to go to the community food shelf to help organize that new donation of canned goods." Bill was the one that kept them organized. In fact, he was sitting at the kitchen table right now, poring over the calendar.

Eric noticed a suspicious red sauce coloring the corner of his friend's mouth. "And what might that be?" he asked in his most imperious tone. Picking up a napkin, he wiped it across Bill's mouth. Confronted with the evidence, Bill smiled mischievously and returned to his calendar.

Eric shrugged and shook his head. "I thought tonight was the political rally," he said.

"Naw, that's tomorrow night."

Deprived of his pizza snack, Eric started to fix dinner. That was his domain. He and Bill shared a comfortable relationship, keeping busy with many good causes. Feeling unwelcome at church, they substituted dishing out meals for the homeless every Sunday and no longer attended church at all. Life was not perfect, but, they reasoned, what other choice did they have?

IF YOU WANT TO EXPLORE THE OTHER CHOICES ERIC COULD HAVE MADE, RETURN TO PAGE 18 OR 173.

O1 ERIC (cont. from page 178)

After seeing a play, Eric and Jackie started walking to a small coffee shop near the theater.

"Oh, Eric, that was great!" she bubbled. "But to be honest, I thought you would never get around to asking me out!"

"You haven't been with the company very long," Eric defended himself.

182

"Some excuse! As of Monday, I will have been there three months."

Eric took her arm and guided her across the street and into the cozy cafe. He was relieved to be seated in a small booth that afforded some privacy. When they were settled, Eric took a deep breath and began to explain. "There was a time, Jackie, when I wouldn't have asked you out," he said.

"Thanks a lot!" she replied, clutching her hand to her heart in mock horror.

"Not because you aren't an attractive woman—because you are," he added quickly. "But being interested in women is something that has been a long, slow process for me."

Jackie leaned her head back against the booth and looked at Eric quizzically. She wasn't sure if he was teasing her or telling the truth. "You're not saying you're gay, are you?"

Eric hated the word *gay*. Struggling with his sexual orientation was anything but a gay or happy experience. "I grew up with a sexual preference for men," he admitted.

"And that's not true now?" Jackie's face mirrored her confusion. "How did you change? I didn't think a homosexual *could* change. I don't understand."

"Whoa, give me a chance. I'll do my best to explain." The waitress brought them two cappuccinos, and Eric was glad for the interruption. It gave him time to gather his thoughts. It wasn't easy telling his dates about his past, but Eric felt it was the only ethical choice he had. They each took a sip of the warm, sweet liquid.

"When I became a Christian, I prayed that God would change me instantly. But he didn't do that. Instead, he led me to a group of Christian homosexuals in an organization called Exodus. They were all people who wanted to live in a way that honored God, but, like me, they weren't attracted to the opposite sex."

"I didn't think gays could be Christian," Jackie replied.

Eric wiped his sweaty palms on his slacks. "There are many homosexuals who love the Lord, but that fact alone doesn't cure them," he said, trying to be patient. "Fortunately, I found a church who welcomed me. They have a support group based on Elizabeth Moberly's concept of developmental deprivation. That really helped." He paused and sipped his drink. "Then I also began private therapy with a Christian counselor who has helped me a lot through prayer and healing."

"And you're cured?" Jackie asked.

"God has used all three—the Exodus group, my church, and my counselors—to help me resolve the issues that affected my orientation and to help me begin looking at a woman as the partner God meant for me to have. It's taken a long time."

"But are you *cured* ?" Jackie asked again.

Eric laughed at her intensity. "I enjoy the company of women now, and someday I hope to marry."

"Good enough," Jackie grinned.

"Does that mean you're still glad I asked you out?"

"You bet," she said.

GO TO PAGE 216 AND LOOK FOR O1

THE MEANING OF "I DO"

Here's what's happening:

2 MICHELLE: Michelle had become a Christian, but long before that she had become mentally detached from her body. What happened to her body didn't matter anymore. And because of that, no one could "get to her." She wanted relationships, but it was so hard to be vulnerable emotionally. If Dad couldn't be trusted, how could other men? She sometimes wondered if she would ever get married.

*** ERIC: Like many with homosexual tendencies, Eric thinks he can "fix" his problem by forcing himself to act in a heterosexual way. He sincerely wants to be attracted to the opposite sex. If you are heterosexual, do you think you could train yourself to be comfortable with a same-sex lover? If you could, do you think it would last forever? Is this the idea God has in mind when he offers us the gift of marriage?

Let's investigate these questions about marriage and then continue Michelle's and Eric's stories.

The Meaning of "I Do"

Miss "You've-come-a-long-way-Baby" and Mr. "With-it" fell in love. After a year's courtship, they decided to get married. They liked the idea of belonging to one another. It simplified insurance coverage and seemed the grown-up thing to do. Their marriage was a social convenience sanctioned by family and friends at a large garden reception at the current "in" spot for such gatherings.

But they missed the point.

You don't have to look any further than Genesis 2:24 to find the origin of marriage. God established it as part of his original design for humankind. In marriage, a man is to *leave* his mother and father (both emotionally and physically) and *cleave* (stick like glue) to his wife. Then husband and wife become *one flesh* (bound together socially, emotionally, and physically) with one another and no one else.

Whenever Jesus spoke of marriage, he always referred to the Genesis definition. He confirmed that God intended marriage to be permanent (Mark 10:7–9) and that it was not simply for procreation. (Childlessness was a common excuse for divorce among the Hebrews. See Matt. 19:9.)

Like many today, Miss "You've-come-a-long-way-Baby" and Mr. "With-it" don't understand that behind the concept of marriage is a divine plan that established two sexes. In Genesis 1:18, God declared that it was "not good" for man to be alone. All the animals paraded before Adam but none of them relieved his loneliness and offered a relationship. So God created Adam's perfect mate from the man's own body. She wasn't just a clone. She was both the same and different. Adam let out a big "a-a-l-l ri-i-ght!" because she was part of him, and their match began a relationship of harmony and loving partnership.

Mankind was declared "good" only after the woman was created. Through their interdependence they were to have children and subdue the earth. Each sex would bring his or her own strengths and weaknesses to the other. Together they would strike the balance of the image of God.

Like other modern couples, Miss "You've-come-a-long-way-Baby" and Mr. "With-it" vowed to stay together "as long as we both shall *love* ." But marriage commitment goes beyond *feelings* of love. Loving feelings naturally come and go. Commitment endures the inevitable ups and downs of marriage in a fallen world. Ideally, couples experience first hand what it means to be loved unconditionally, exemplifying the Father's love. And, in the passion of intercourse practiced within a trusting, lasting, relationship, they drop the fences around their egos and become one flesh.

God celebrates monogamous marriage between men and women as the best possible environment to raise children and carry out his work. No modern reinterpretation (certainly not social convenience marriages or those who say they don't need a piece of paper to have a committed relationship) has proven sounder or healthier for physical, emotional, or spiritual development. God created children to need the influence and stability of two parents who work as a team. "Woman is not independent of man, nor is man independent of woman' (1 Cor. 11:11).

If we want to live wisely, it makes sense to stick to the instructions of the person who designed the system.

What happens next:

■2 MICHELLE (cont. from page 185)

"Whoa, break time!" Tom unwrapped himself from Michelle's arms and tried to cool off. "You're one beautiful lady, Michelle, but sex, before marriage, in a car, with someone I'm just getting to know isn't part of my plan," he said nervously. "It just doesn't fit in with my Christianity."

Michelle sat up angrily. "Hey, I'm a Christian, too!" she shot back.

Tom shifted and leaned back against the driver's door. "I'm not questioning that, Michelle. But as single Christians we can't get sexually involved." He sighed and went on. "You know, I find you very appealing," he said, tenderly brushing her hair back from her eyes. "So if I plan to stick to God's best for me, I'm going to have to be super careful around you."

Michelle swallowed hard, trying to hide her hurt. "No other Christian man I've dated bothered to be so holier-than-thou!" Folding her arms, she stared straight ahead, not wanting him to see the tears in her eyes.

Tom took her hand and gave it a little squeeze. "I'm sorry that's been your experience with other Christian guys. I know other guys do it. Not having sex before marriage is extremely difficult— especially with a wonderful girl like you."

Michelle jerked her hand back. "I want out!" she exploded, tearing at the locked door to make a hasty exit.

Tom reached over and put his arms around her, holding her tightly against his chest. "I didn't mean to hurt you," he said softly.

"Better let me go. You might get 'horny.'"

"I'm sorry that you're angry and hurt, Michelle. Shall we talk about it?" He released her slowly, and they sat quietly for a few minutes.

Michelle dug through her purse looking for a tissue. Tom propped his hand on the steering wheel and waited patiently while she blew her nose.

Clearly this man was different. Despite her ugly words and overreaction, she felt no judgment from him. He offered only unconditional love. Maybe she could risk being honest with him. "I've never known any other way to be with a man," she admitted. "From the time I was a little girl, men have wanted one thing from me. I know how to please them."

"But pleasing men is not your goal as a Christian, right? Pleasing God is," Tom reminded her.

"That sounds so simple, Tom. But I'm used to having sex with men I have a relationship with. It's a habit." Michelle looked for a negative reaction in Tom's eyes but there was none.

Tom smiled reassuringly. "When you became a Christian, you stopped being a slave to your behavior," he said gently. "You have the Holy Spirit to help you be free." He ran the back of his hand over her cheek. "I know a woman in our church you could talk to. I think she would be a real help."

Michelle melted. "Tom, I'm sorry I got so mad," she said. "I really like you, and I want you to like me. I just thought you would want to have sex with me."

His eyes searched hers compassionately. "If you didn't like me, you might have had sex with me, too," he ventured. "I think some people do it just to feel powerful or because they can't think of anything else to do."

Michelle knew he was right but couldn't say anything.

"Sex is not meant to be used as a reward for ourselves or others," Tom reminded her. "And it's not just a game to pass the time." He sighed and reached to start the car.

Michelle scooted over to him and leaned her head on his shoulder. "What did you say that lady's name was?" she asked.

Tom's friend was a help to Michelle. She, too, had been molested. Michelle began to understand how her promiscuous lifestyle was related to being a victim. More importantly, she began to understand how to have and maintain healthy relationships with the opposite sex.

GO TO PAGE 157 AND LOOK FOR ■2

⁎⁎ ERIC (cont. from page 185)

Our society places a lot of emphasis on getting married. Somehow taking a wife or husband suddenly is supposed to make a person mature, smarter, or more settled. Rarely do churches give singles positions of leadership. Getting married is the cure for what ails you—or so people think. Will it really solve Eric's problem, or will it just increase the number of people he hurts? Make a choice for Eric:

⁎⁎1 Eric has developed doubts about pursuing a girlfriend and marriage. He thinks it would be unfair to the woman he would marry.

GO TO PAGE 191 AND LOOK FOR ⁎⁎1

.2 Eric decides that marriage will cure his homosexual feelings. Then he'll be straight, and the marriage will be okay. He looks for a girl to marry.

GO TO PAGE 204 AND LOOK FOR **.2

SEXUAL IMMORALITY

Here's what's happening:

**2 MICHELLE: People often choose to be sexual for other than sexual reasons. Michelle was one of them. She used sex to humiliate, demonstrate her power, and massage her ego. It is a mistake to think that most sexual immorality occurs because people can't resist the powerful sensations.

**1 ERIC: Eric decides to search Scripture for guidance in how men and women are to live their sexual lives. He is surprised at how clear the guidelines in 1 Thessalonians 4 are, and he begins to understand what sexual immorality really means.

O ERIC: Some people do wrong because they have never heard what's right. Eric was fortunate that good people cared enough about him to tell him the truth.

Michelle and Eric, like all of us, need to know what sexual immorality really is—and what it does. Let's talk about it, and then we'll return to their stories.

Sexual Immorality

Despite what *Playboy* or Madison Avenue would have us believe, sex was God's idea first. He designed us to be the sexy creatures we are, curiously omitting a switch to turn off our sexual feelings. How much simpler life would be if we had one! God expects us to accept what we are—sexy and capable of living that way morally.

He made sex a seal of a man and woman's determination to spend their life together. Nothing can replace it—not a written contract, or hiking the Himalayas together, or even advertising your commitment in *The New York Times* . Giving your body to another (especially for the first time) is such a vulnerable, profound thing that its significance goes beyond words. That's what God intended. It symbolizes the deepest commitment possible, which becomes even richer as a couple builds a shared history.

Today, however, many people view sex as simply a natural expression of physical desires. It doesn't make sense to them to reserve it for marriage even though it is the most personal and private aspect of life. Their motto is: If it feels good, do it.

But sex with everybody becomes sex with nobody. The *most* these people can say is, "It felt good." And their pleasure is nothing compared to the pleasure of those who reserve their gift of sex for expression within a special, committed, life-long relationship.

Others hinge their sexual activity on affection. Sex is the way they tell others they care for them. Some even seek sexual relationships to prove that they themselves are lovable. But there are many other ways to express love, and the physical version is often the least caring, especially when life plans are disrupted by unplanned pregnancy, health damaged by STDs (Sexually Transmitted Diseases), and emotions trampled when the rest of the relationship can't equal the importance of sex.

Sexual immorality is choosing to use sex in ways it was never designed for. Its results are superficial and sometimes painful. God calls us to be sexually responsible people because he invented sex and wants us to enjoy it at its best. He knows that if we ignore his plan for sexuality, we'll miss out on the pleasure, depth, and oneness that we can experience when we follow his guidelines.

Sexual immorality specifically refers to fornication, adultery, prostitution, incest, bestiality, and homosexuality. These are listed by name in the Bible as immoral sexual behavior. God tells us to "flee from sexual immorality. All other sins a man commits are outside his body, but he who sins sexually sins against his own body" (1 Cor. 6:18). Other activities can also be immoral depending on our motives: Are we loving our neighbor as ourselves?

"It is God's will that you should be holy; that you should avoid sexual immorality" (1 Thess. 4:3). But how? Verse four gives a clue: "Each of you should learn to control his own body." If you want to accept God's gift of sex and use it the way it was intended, first analyze what turns you on sexually and in what situations you are vulnerable. As the verse implies, for each of us this will be different. Learn your vulnerable areas and devise a plan to avoid them.

Second, don't let the world set the standard for what is appropriate sexual behavior for you. No matter what your favorite movie star does or the latest teen movie suggests, follow what is right for you before God. (See v. 5.)

Finally, remember that the Lord promises judgment upon anyone who takes advantage of another person sexually (v. 6). Sexual exploitation is possible whenever there is an inappropriate difference in age, emotional maturity, or social development: a teacher who seduces a student, a sixteen-year-old who encourages a four-year-old to manipulate his or her genitals, a boy who convinces his girlfriend that he loves her so she will be intimate. Even if both appear to be willing participants, it can still be sexual exploitation.

God doesn't declare certain sexual behavior off limits because he's a killjoy or enjoys throwing difficult tests our way. He loves us and wants us to experience the best. No one questions that living purely is difficult in a fallen world, but it's not impossible either.

Both the Bible and reality teach that designing our own path always has its consequences. David *chose* to commit adultery with Bathsheba. Although he received forgiveness, the repercussions of his sexual immorality included murder, the weakening of his kingdom, the death of one son, and the rebellion and eventual death of another. Asking for forgiveness and receiving it doesn't wipe out the consequences of our actions.

The wise person follows the manufacturer's instructions for minimum problems and maximum pleasure—especially when the chief designer is the Lord!

What happens next?

**2 MICHELLE (cont. from page 191)

Michelle sat with Kay and Miriam at the back lunch table in the cafeteria, picking at their sloppy joes and killing time before the bell. Michelle kept pointing to various boys around the room and telling the other girls some little quirk, bad habit, or private bit of gossip about each one.

"Danny didn't really do that, did he?" Kay asked, adding an incredulous squeal that brought stares from classmates at nearby tables.

"You wanna bet?" replied Michelle, holding up her right hand with great seriousness. "But the real news is about Bobbie Green—you know, Macho Stud? Well, he was so overpowered by the charms of yours truly that he wasn't even able to make it to the starting line."

"No!" Kay's eyes grew wide. "He must have died of embarrassment!"

"I loved it," Michelle said with a laugh. Then she noticed that Miriam wasn't laughing. "What's wrong with you?" she asked. "He deserved it and you know it."

Miriam looked disgusted. "Don't you ever get tired of making it with guys you don't even like?" she asked. Miriam had often heard Michelle recounting her weekend "sexploits." Although Miriam was no angel herself, these cold-blooded Monday morning dissections were really getting to her.

"Listen, Miriam. Boys are just wimps when it comes to sex,"

Michelle told her. "There's not one of them that I can't have eating out of my hand if I have enough time and the right setting."

Just then the bell rang, and Michelle gladly got caught up in the usual pandemonium. Something about Miriam's question was more unsettling than the sloppy joe.

Michelle had never heard of sex as a means of bringing two people closer, as a seal on a commitment, or as anything more than momentary pleasure.

GO TO PAGE 135 AND LOOK FOR **2

**1 ERIC (cont. from page 191)

"Carol, I never meant to hurt you." Eric would have given his life not to have caused her such pain and horror. Yes, horror was there, too—all over Carol's face.

It was a hot day, and they had gone out to the mountains about an hour out of town for a relaxing afternoon picnic. Neither had eaten much. They lost their appetite when Eric confessed that his love for Carol wasn't the kind that could include marriage.

"What a fool I've been," she said bitterly. "I thought you were different from other boys and didn't try anything because you respected me." She paused. "I didn't know you were *repulsed* by me."

"I'm not repulsed by you or any other girl," Eric tried to explain. "I'm sure that if we married, I would be able to have sex with you. But I've been reading Song of Solomon lately, trying to understand God's model for sexual love between men and women. And I have to admit my feelings for you don't fit."

"I don't understand, Eric."

Even when she frowned, she looked beautiful, Eric thought. He liked it when she pulled her hair back in a french braid. "I don't understand it either." He lay back on the rock, seeking solace from the warm rays of the sun.

Regaining her composure, Carol began using her sharp problem-solving skills to find a way out. "Have you asked God to change you?" she asked. "Surely this doesn't have to be—"

"I have asked, begged, and threatened, but God's answer is apparently, 'Not now.'" He rolled over and looked at the gorgeous mountains God had created. "I don't doubt for a minute that God is almighty," he said. "He *can* change me. But it has to be in his timing."

"What about counseling?" Carol wouldn't give up easily. "God sometimes heals through other people."

"I've been that route, too."

Carol moved over by him and put her arm across his back. The lump in Eric's throat prevented him from telling her how much he needed her to touch him. He was so afraid of total rejection.

Finally Eric broke the silence. "God has answered one prayer about this," he said. "He let me know without a doubt that marrying you to 'fix' my sexual orientation would be taking advantage of you sexually. And that's a sin."

"Sin always has consequences," Carol added.

"You got it." Propping himself up on his elbow, he looked directly at her. "This is painful for both of us now, but it's nothing compared to what would be waiting for us down the road."

"What are you going to do?" asked Carol.

"Well, to be honest, sometimes I'm tempted to enter a homosexual relationship. But I know that's not the solution either. For now, I'm going to keep trusting that remaining single is God's best for me."

GO TO PAGE 198 AND LOOK FOR ⁑1

O ERIC (cont. from page 191)
Eric goes to a youth rally at a friend's church. The minister gives a sermon on Jesus' love for all human beings. Eric hears for the first time that Jesus loved him enough to die for him, not because Eric was perfect but because he was a sinner. Eric accepts Jesus as his personal Savior. How will knowing the Lord make a difference in Eric's life? Will he stop having feelings for males because he is a new person in Christ? Choose one for Eric:

○1. Eric understands that acting on his homosexual feelings is sin. He prays for the Lord to miraculously take away his desire for men.
GO TO PAGE 178 AND LOOK FOR ○1

○2. Although Eric would like a miraculous healing, his prayer is more modest; he asks God to show him how to live in a way that will honor him. He also asks God to provide the strength to do it.
GO TO PAGE 170 AND LOOK FOR ○2

A PRACTICAL PLAN FOR SINGLES

Here's what's happening:

■1 JASON: Jason had always heard that "women say no but mean yes" and that if you didn't act on your sexual desires, you got something called "blue balls," which wasn't healthy. His friends said that anyone who didn't do what came naturally was inhibited. Then Jason learned that a person can live a healthy, normal life without being sexually active. Being in charge of his sex life instead of it being in charge of him was a new concept.

**1 ERIC: Eric has already concluded that trying to "fix" his homosexual tendencies through relationships with females is wrong; now, he determines to keep himself pure and sets about to find God's perfect plan for his sexuality.

Both Jason and Eric have decided to control their sex lives; let's discuss how that's done, and then we'll continue their stories.

A Practical Plan for Singles

Most current television programs, movies, books, and magazines have a common message: (1) You will go crazy if you don't act on your sexual desires, and (2) self-discipline is equally unhealthy. Take heart. Singles are not asked to maintain singleness at the risk of their sanity! Being a virgin is normal.

You can count on God to help. "For it is God who works in you to will and to act according to his good purpose" (Phil. 2:13). If he was willing to die for you, there is no question of his being available through the tough temptations of single life. Remember the motto: When it's bigger than I am, so is God.

He is the Truth and the Way. The Bible clearly teaches that the fullest expression of our sexuality is reserved for marriage. So what can single people do about the fact that, like married people, they desire physical expression of their love? They have several choices.

First, they could repress their drive, but there are some problems with that. Those who try to turn off sexual feelings may find, to their surprise, that they turn back on with a rush at a most vulnerable time. Not having faced the strong emotions of the situation, the person is easily overwhelmed, letting the body rule. And letting the body rule is prohibited in the Bible.

Repression can also decrease people's ability to recognize and respond to their natural sexual feelings even when the setting is appropriate. Sex counselors deal with this problem daily.

For Christians, successfully repressing sexual feelings can lead to a holier-than-thou attitude. Never lose sight of the individual nature of our physical responses. Those who have little trouble handling their sexual nature may have the gift of singleness, and they should consider whether God has some special plans for them in using the gift (1 Cor. 7:7).

A less powerful form of repression is suppression or its close cousin, sublimation. It's not 100 percent effective, but some people convert sexual drive into energy used for work, creative pursuits, study, and sports. There is nothing unhealthful about the process, and it's probably the most widely practiced means of controlling one's sex drive.

Another somewhat successful method is to develop a network of friends who add meaning and dimension to life, a body of fellow-Christians who provide support, caring, and depth. This only works if you face the issue of sex firmly and honestly sometime in the relationships. To deny that sexual feelings exist, even between the most unlikely of our opposite-sex friends, is to risk being caught unawares.

Remember, the feeling isn't the problem. Failing to face the emotion is. Then you deny yourself the opportunity to make insightful and healthy decisions about your course of action. We don't find ourselves in sticky situations by accident. We get there through a series of conscious or unconscious yeses. Rich relationships that don't include sex are possible. Jesus modeled them for us.

No reinterpretation of the Bible that can justify other outlets, such as sex with other singles, adultery, or homosexuality. The Bible does promise that when we accept Christ, we become new creatures. Our old ways are gone (2 Cor. 5:17). Don't ever forget that your major resource for dealing with sexual drives is the Lord. God will always be with you, perhaps supernaturally helping you live with yourself and moving you toward the person he wants you to become.

A proper mindset is essential. You may need to reject most of the popular music of the day, many of the movies, the suggestive clothing, and videos. That takes a Herculean effort, especially if you weren't raised with correct moral values or weren't taught why the evils were labeled off limits. When you are encouraged to stand up for your personal beliefs, you'll be able to think clearly and manage your sex life wisely.

If you follow all these suggestions and your sex drive still threatens to send you to the showers three times a day, perhaps the answer is occasional masturbation with your mind focused on thanking God for a body capable of pleasurable response. Claim the promises that, "to the pure, all things are pure" (Tit. 1:15) and "everything God created is good, and nothing is to be rejected if it is received with thanksgiving" (1 Tim. 4:4).

200

Avoiding immoral behavior is never easy. You can't count on much praise or support. It takes a decision, a plan, personal awareness, and trust. Remember, the things you're missing out on (herpes, genital warts, unplanned pregnancies, broken hearts, lowered self-esteem, the spoiling of new relationships with memories of old ones) are worth missing.

What happens next?

■1 JASON (cont. from page 198)

JASON (cont. from page 198)

Jason and Suzy entered their room laughing, kicked off their shoes, and fell on the bed together, hugging each other tightly. They had just gotten home from celebrating their first wedding anniversary. Their three-year courtship had culminated with a lovely ceremony performed by the youth pastor who had been helpful in the early days of their romance.

Suzy's green eyes twinkled as she looked lovingly at her husband. "Jason, you know what made me happiest tonight?" she asked.

Jason curled a lock of her long brown hair around his finger. "Let me guess," he teased. "My wonderful gift?"

"No."

He sat up, crossing his legs in front of him, Indian style. "Getting a piece of cake with a flower on it all to yourself?"

She giggled. "No—but that's a close second!"

"I give up," he replied with mock frustration.

Suzy sat up facing him. "Your dad toasting us and saying how good we are for one another." Tears glistened in her eyes as she recalled the moment. "Miracles never cease. The things he said were really special." They both knew that Jason's dad was not at all sure about "this Christian thing." Yet the obvious love and respect within their marriage had been a good witness.

Jason nodded thoughtfully. "You know how Dad always used to ask me about my sex life when I was a teenager? Well, tonight he got me alone and asked if our sex life had been worth the wait."

Suzy gasped. "He didn't!"

"He sure did. I guess old habits are sometimes hard to break. I started to tell him it was none of his business or sock him playfully in the arm like we used to do, but I decided to talk to him straight— kinda like you did on one of our early dates."

"And—?"

"I told him that waiting had given us the greatest gift we could give to one another—the exclusive right to the other's body, sealed morally and legally by the marriage ceremony. I also told him that since we are both very sensuous people, we enjoy sex immensely and frequently, and we're always open to new ways of being together that make us feel like we're one and secure in our love."

"Did he understand?"

"I'm not sure," Jason replied. "When you've been brought up thinking sex is only a physical act, it's hard to imagine the meaning and freedom it can have in a committed relationship. When you only know the moves and not the meaning, you have to direct a lot of energy toward looking for new partners or techniques that promise to keep sex good."

Touched by her husband's sensitivity, Suzy knelt down by the bed to pray. Jason quickly joined her, and together they thanked God for the richness and joy in their marriage, for the physical relationship so important to them, and for the trust they have in each other and God's love. Then they made love.

IF YOU WANT TO EXPLORE OTHER CHOICES JASON COULD HAVE MADE, RETURN TO PAGE 14 OR 104.

✳✳1 ERIC (cont. from page 198)

A few years later. . .

Eric spotted Carol as soon as he walked into the restaurant. He waved and hurried over to greet her. "Carol, I couldn't believe it was you when you called. How long are you going to be in town?"

"Two days. I'm here on some family business, and I heard you were living here, so I wanted to say hi." She was as youthful looking as she had been that day in the mountains.

Eric was genuinely glad to see her. "I'm so glad you did," he said. "And I'm glad I was able to get away during my lunch break. How long has it been, anyway?" he asked.

"Seven years," Carol said, raising her eyebrows. "Of course, there've been a few changes." She patted her bulging tummy and chuckled.

Just then the hostess came and showed them to their table.

Once settled, Carol looked across the table and smiled. "It's been so long since we've been in touch," she said. "But I've prayed for you. Has God answered your prayer?"

"I guess God's answer is still Wait, but he is faithful. The temptations have been great, yet I've been able to remain morally responsible." A smile crossed his face as he remembered Carol's arm around him that traumatic day when he told her they would have to end their relationship. Not everyone he shared with had been so understanding! He nodded toward her stomach. "When's the baby due?"

"Two more months," she said proudly. "It's our first. God has been faithful to me, too. I thought I would never get over not being able to marry you—" She looked away briefly, then smiled. "But then along came John." She shook her napkin out and looked for a lap to set it on. Catching Eric's eye, she started laughing, and he quickly joined in.

After a moment Eric grew serious again. "I have to be very careful about my relationships with certain men," he admitted. "But I've developed some good friendships with women now. The important thing is that I control my sexual desires, that they don't control me."

"I heard you have a great job and you're involved in a lot of projects for your church."

"I have nothing to complain about," Eric replied. And he meant it. He hadn't resolved all his problems, but he found a certain peace in trusting God for his timing and in knowing he was moving in the right direction.

IF YOU WANT TO EXPLORE OTHER CHOICES ERIC COULD HAVE MADE, RETURN TO PAGE 18 OR 189.

THE DIVORCE DECISION: WILL IT EVER END?

Here's what's happening:

**2 ERIC: Eric is sure that Cindy, a strong Christian he met at church, can help him overcome his feelings for other men. She is attractive and appreciates the fact that Eric hasn't pressured her for sex, like so many men have. After they marry, she wishes they would be intimate more frequently, but she realizes that Eric is under pressure, juggling work and the classes he takes at college. Two years later they have a baby boy, and Eric confesses his attraction to men. Cindy can't handle it—she files for divorce.

Divorce has consequences for everyone involved. We'll continue Eric's story as soon as we've talked about some of those consequences.

The Divorce Decision: Will It Ever End?

No one ever marries expecting that it will end in divorce. Marriage was designed to be permanent. In Matthew 19:6 Jesus refers to the original plan, the ideal of *one flesh*. "What God has joined together," he warns, "let man not separate." The family was meant to be a secure unit which provided the best environment for raising children (two parents of opposite sex, in a dependable, committed union).

You don't have to be a psychologist or social worker to see what happens when marriages don't follow the original plan. On a scale of life's most stressful events, divorce is second only to death of a spouse. Children of divorced parents often go through years of adjustment problems. There is a higher suicide rate among kids from broken homes, but even those who don't take their lives have unfortunately quit believing in a "happily ever after." According to statistics, the likelihood of a person getting divorced is considerably greater if his or her parents have divorced.

Divorce rarely brings out the best in people. It leads otherwise mature men and women to behaviors, rages, and jealousies they never imagined they were capable of. Financially, it cripples most people for years. Today the lawyers' fees alone can total $15,000 for an average California couple. Some people divorce in hopes of finding something better. But actually, second marriages only have a 30 percent survival rate.

Jesus said that the Old Testament permitted divorce in some cases because of people's hard hearts. In a world where sin exists, the ideal human living arrangement often gets distorted. Although many people debate the appropriateness of divorce, there appear to be three situations where divorce is understandable: adultery, abuse, and abandonment.

Trust is so vital to marriage that the Lord understands the major wound caused when adultery violates that trust.

In the case of abuse, Ephesians 5:25 says that husbands are to love their wives as Christ loves the Church. Christ never treats the Church in a life-threatening or emotionally battering fashion. A warped relationship can become so detrimental that unhinging it seems the only humane thing to do.

In the case of abandonment, the spouse who leaves completely relinquishes his or her role and rejects the marital vows. A marriage in name only is no marriage.

Leaving, however, was never intended to be taken lightly. Sensing the seriousness of divorce, Jesus' disciples suggested that it was better not to marry, than to marry and divorce. Jesus reminded them that men and women were designed to desire one another, so most people will want to marry. Only a few, who have the gift of singleness will be comfortable not marrying.

Much of the social stigma that kept marriages together in the past is gone. While opinions on divorce and remarriage differ widely among churches, generally more churches now accept the modern tendency to leave one marriage and begin anew.

Sometimes the odds of an ailing marriage recovering look slim. But reconciliation often depends more on the individuals involved than the types of problems they face. As a marriage counselor, I have seen some couples who couldn't overcome rather minor disagreements while others worked through seemingly unsurmountable odds.

For example, Sondra and Jay had been married twelve years. Sondra did not believe in divorce but had reached the point in their emotionally sterile marriage where it seemed the only option. She had tried everything to make her husband understand how starved she was for emotional intimacy with him.

Jay kept all his concerns bottled up and busied himself with many good causes. Until Sondra took the risk of asking for a separation, Jay didn't realize how much his family meant to him. Finally he entered counseling and began to look at some old issues from his childhood that prevented him from being vulnerable and emotionally intimate with anyone—including his wife.

When Jay wanted to move back in, Sondra wasn't eager to let him. Convinced that all her feelings for Jay had been trampled under his insensitivity, she no longer felt she had the emotional energy left for a new start. With no enthusiasm but an obedient heart, she agreed to a once-a-week "date," but it was his responsibility to arrange it in a way that would demonstrate his increasing sensitivity to her.

Each week they were also to exchange letters which honestly shared their fears, desires, and hopes. Restoration of this marriage was a long and often disheartening process. Sondra wisely refused to reenter the marriage until they both were convinced that their relationship would be a new one. To symbolize this, they burned pieces of paper on which they had written their deepest emotional hurts from their "old" union. And before Jay returned to the home, they sealed their "new" union with a new marriage ceremony.

Recovery was possible because Jay faced the issues that prevented him from being the kind of husband God called him to be. Sondra's evaluation that "nothing was left" motivated her to be open to the Lord's power to do what on the human level seemed impossible. Despite her feelings, she continued to participate in their "dates" and counseling.

Divorce can be avoided to a large degree if the couple understands that marriage is forever and if they make the effort to give it its rightful priority. If you're considering marriage, you should go through a dating and/or engagement seminar or extensive marriage counseling. How people handle problems tells a lot about their character. If you decide not to marry, it may be a sad decision, but the pain is minor compared to a possible lifetime of recovery from divorce.

What happens next?

**2 ERIC (cont. from page 204)

Almost a year later. . .

Eric passed Mr. Springsted's new car in the law firm's parking lot. Mr. Springsted had been Eric's friend and lawyer ever since the divorce proceedings began, but Eric couldn't help but wonder if the fees from the long, drawn-out legal battle had paid for this fine vehicle.

As the receptionist ushered Eric into his attorney's office, Mr. Springsted smiled uneasily. "Thanks for coming, Eric," he said kindly.

Eric bit his lip. He wanted to say something about the new car but refused to give in to bitterness. Eric nodded and said, "Hi, I'm surprised to see you so soon," he said. "The court proceedings were just two weeks ago."

Mr. Springsted motioned for Eric to have a seat. "I'm sorry you had to come in." He wasted no time getting down to business.

"I warned you, Eric, about the futility of trying to get custody. Gays rarely get custody of their children after a divorce."

"But I'm the most stable parent," Eric protested. "Cindy has been in and out of alcohol treatment centers and sometimes can't even take care of herself."

"As you know, many people feel you are responsible for putting her in that position," Mr. Springsted replied matter-of-factly.

"Well, that's their problem," he said defensively. "No matter who I like to go to bed with, no one can deny that I love my son. Nobody can say I'm not a good father."

"At the moment Cindy's folks are in the driver's seat," the lawyer told him. "They have custody until Cindy is stronger. They have filed a petition asking the court to deny you visitation rights."

"They can't do that!" Eric exploded. He jumped up and started pacing the floor. "They just can't do that to me!"

"They have."

Eric stopped pacing and leaned his hands on Mr. Springsted's desk. "On what grounds?" he asked, looking the lawyer right in the eye.

"Apparently you've had a string of male visitors at your apartment. They've had a private detective watching you."

Eric's knees buckled and he sunk into a chair. It was true. Since the divorce, he had thrown aside any hesitancy about indulging in the homosexual lifestyle and made up for lost time. The visitors to the apartment were just the tip of the iceberg. Most of his encounters took place in bars, bathhouses, and bathrooms.

"What can I do?" he asked meekly.

"Pray a lot," replied Mr. Springsted, only half seriously.

But Eric had forgotten how to pray.

GO TO PAGE 209 AND LOOK FOR ⁑2

SEXUALLY TRANSMITTED DISEASES

Here's what's happening:

○2 JASON: Eventually Jason is open to almost any sexual practice or partner if it promises something new. *Only other people get sexually transmitted diseases*, he tells himself. Jason doesn't worry. Should he?

✳✳2 ERIC: Because of Eric's immaturity, he did whatever he wanted for the pleasure of the moment without considering the consequences. This complicated his relationships and alienated him from his son. It also put him at physical risk— his "safe-sex" practices were almost nonexistent.

What are the risks of careless sex? We'll talk about it, and then continue with Jason's and Eric's stories.

Sexually Transmitted Diseases

Once upon a time there was a land where the most fearful thing that could happen as a result of unprotected intercourse was pregnancy. That land was located somewhere between the invention of penicillin and the discovery of AIDS. It no longer exists.

The AIDS virus destroys the body's immune system. Many people carry the virus and pass it on to others but do not develop the disease themselves. As of the summer of 1988, it was estimated that 1.5 million people in the United States had been infected with the Human Immunodeficiency virus (HIV). Of these 1.5 million, 40,000 now have AIDS or AIDS-related illnesses, and 25,000 have already died. Even if a cure were found tomorrow, a great number of people would still become ill with the disease in the next five to ten years.

By 1991, there will be approximately 179,000 people sick or dying of AIDS with the cost of their care estimated at 8.5 billion dollars. AIDS will then be the leading cause of death among people 25–40 years old.

AIDS is more prevalent among gays, bisexual men, people who share IV needles, and sex partners of these groups. Carried in body fluids, the virus may enter the body through a break in the lining of the rectum, through the vagina or mouth, or through a needle puncture.

Some AIDS symptoms (swollen glands, fever, night sweats, severe fatigue, and weight loss) are similar to those of other diseases—except that AIDS symptoms don't go away. They only get worse. Currently there is no cure for AIDS. Death is inevitable.

Unfortunately, AIDS is such a major health threat that many resources have been diverted away from the many other STDs. Most of those can be treated, some can only be controlled, *but all can be prevented.*

HOW DO YOU KNOW IF YOU HAVE A SEXUALLY TRANSMITTED DISEASE?

If you are not sexually active, you can't get a sexually transmitted disease. If you are sexually active, you're susceptible no matter what your race, occupation, or sexual preference. Men become aware that they are infected more easily than women because they have more obvious physical symptoms. Because symptoms may come and go, their absence does not mean the person is cured. Some common symptoms include:

1. *Discharge* : In men, a white or clear (often thick) discharge from the penis—or from the rectum if infected during anal sex. In

210

women, an unusual discharge, often accompanied by itching, burning, or odor.

2. *Burning.* Occurs frequently with urination.

3. *Lumps and bumps.* Skin changes near the genitals.

4. *Abdominal pain.* In women this could be an indication of Pelvic Inflammatory Disease (PID), a condition that can lead to chronic pelvic infections, loss of babies, and difficulty in getting pregnant.

5. *Itching.* In both sexes itching around the sex organs may be a sign of herpes, scabies, or crabs. Women may itch due to vaginitis (which isn't always the result of sexual activity).

6. *Sores.* Located on or near the sex organs.

7. *No symptoms.* Especially in women, symptoms may take years to develop. If there is any possibility of exposure, consult a doctor before permanent damage is done.

WHAT SHOULD YOU DO IF YOU HAVE A SEXUALLY TRANSMITTED DISEASE?

Get medical treatment as soon as possible. Although you can legally get treatment without your parents knowing, it is wise to seek their counsel. Without prompt treatment for you and your partner(s), serious complications can result.

Don't take a friend's old medicines, but do take all your medication and check back with your doctor to see if you are cured.

WHAT IS THE RISK OF GETTING A SEXUALLY TRANSMITTED DISEASE?

If you are not sexually active, you have no risk of getting an STD. If the person you marry has also been sexually pure, you will never have to deal with any complications of sexual diseases. However, if a woman, for example, has been sexually pure and her spouse has had four partners previous to her, he has subjected her to increased infections and multiplied her risk of cervical cancer severalfold. Risk increases considerably with each new sexual partner. So-called "safe sex" is not *safe*—it's merely *safer*. Abstaining is the only form of safe sex that exits.

WHAT ARE THE MOST COMMON SEXUALLY TRANSMITTED DISEASES?

There are approximately thirty types of STDs. The one that is spreading the fastest in people 15–25 is *chlamydia*. It is particularly worrisome because it is often symptomless. Untreated, it can cause sterility in both males and females.

First symptoms in women often indicate Pelvic Inflammatory Disease (PID), a leading cause of tubal pregnancies, infertility, pain during sex, and abdominal pain. A woman with chlamydia can give her newborn baby infections that can result in the baby's death.

There are some new tests to detect chlamydia and medicines to treat it, hopefully before secondary problems begin.

AIDS is by far the deadliest STD, but *herpes* has been known to affect people's lives greatly—so much so that support groups for people who live with the disease have sprung up throughout the country. Like AIDS, there is no cure. Symptoms, which most often include painful blisters and sores on the genitals or mouth, come and go (though not all such sores indicate that a person has the STD). A drug called Acyclovir speeds up healing in some herpes sufferers and may reduce occurrences. Herpes can be spread even before an active sore appears. A baby born to a mother with herpes can have severe complications or die.

Venereal warts, like chlamydia, is a relatively new STD. These warts are so tiny that they often aren't easily detected, but their effect can be significant. There is much evidence linking venereal warts to cervical cancer, and newborn babies can contract them from their mothers.

Warts are removed several ways—chemically, surgically, or through freezing. The smaller they are, the easier the treatment. Sometimes repeated treatment is necessary.

Vaginitis can be sexually spread or it can occur naturally. Trichomoniasis, yeast infection, and gardnerella are the most common types. Trichomoniasis is often passed back and forth between partners.

The most common symptom is a discharge specific to each infection. Treatment can include oral medication, creams, and/or suppositories. Women subject to such infections should be careful

212

to wash with soap and water daily, avoid douches or strong deodorant soap, and wear cotton-crotch undergarments.

Both *gonorrhea* and *syphilis* have been around for generations, and those who get prompt treatment with antibiotics can be cured. Men usually have a discharge and painful urination, but women often do not know they are infected until serious damage has been done to internal organs. Gonorrhea can cause sterility and PID.

Syphilis is frightening because the first symptom, a painless sore followed later by a rash and by fever, disappear, leaving a false sense of security. Years later the infection reappears with more serious consequences which can be untreatable and lead to death. After a decade of decline, syphilis is on the rise again.

What happens next?

○2 JASON (cont. from page 209)

Several years later. . .

Exhausted from lack of sleep, Jason sank into a vinyl chair in the small examining room at the hospital and listened intently to his baby's doctor.

"I'm sorry, Jason," the doctor told him. "There is no question. Your baby has AIDS and is very sick." He reached out and touched Jason softly on the shoulder. "We don't expect him to live more than twenty-four hours."

Jason's hands trembled. His precious son, barely a month old, would be dead by tomorrow! He placed his head in his hands and wept. "How could this be, Doc? I'm not gay. I don't use drugs!" More than anything in his life Jason wanted to hear that it was all a mistake.

"It's AIDS, Jason. Since neither you nor Stacy has ever had a blood transfusion, I would guess it was picked up from a prostitute. Could that be possible?"

Jason shuddered. Since his marriage to Stacy he had cut down on his visits to prostitutes. He wasn't quite as wild as he had been in high school and college. And because he had been discreet about his behavior, most people viewed him as a happily married man.

"My wife was frigid," he said with a shrug. "I went out a few times to get my needs met," he lied. Jason remembered how shocked Stacy had been when she found out about his "visits" and his love of pornography. For a while she tried to pretend it didn't matter. But Jason always knew it did.

Jason looked up quickly. "What about Stacy?" he asked. "Does she have AIDS, too?"

The doctor leaned against the examining table, his face filled with compassion. "She tests positive for the HIV virus," he said frankly. "She may or may not develop the full disease."

As tears ran down Jason's cheeks, somehow the small examining room seemed even smaller and more sterile than before.

The doctor wheeled a small stool over and sat down. "And Jason," he said, trying to cushion his words with kindness, "of course, you also are HIV positive."

How could Jason have known it would all end up like this?

IF YOU WANT TO EXPLORE OTHER CHOICES JASON COULD HAVE MADE, RETURN TO PAGE 14 OR 138.

✻✻2 ERIC (cont. from page 209)

A couple years later. . .

"Good morning, Eric." His mother entered his room with her usual routine—the one he remembered from childhood. She would greet him, open the drapes, pull up the blinds, and sit for a few minutes on the edge of his bed. Who would have thought that she would still be going through that routine when he was twenty-six years old!

Eric lifted a splotchy and emaciated arm and took his mother's hand. "Mom, it's really nice of you and Dad to let me come home," he said.

"Well, Eric—" She placed her other hand over his. "—you're our son, and you need us."

"I couldn't believe it when they kicked me out of the apartment," he said weakly.

She stood to leave. "Never mind," she said. "Don't worry. Just think of getting well."

Eric didn't let go of her hand. "Mom, I'm sorry for all the years you didn't hear much from me."

Without a reply she sat down again and reached into her apron pocket for a note she had placed there. "Oh, yes, your lawyer called," she told him. "He thinks he has made a breakthrough in your humanitarian petition to see your son. He's sorry it's taken so long, but he says to hang in there."

But Eric couldn't hang in there. The morning the court approved a visit with his son, he died of AIDS.

IF YOU WANT TO EXPLORE OTHER CHOICES ERIC COULD HAVE MADE, RETURN TO PAGE 18 OR 189.

FORGIVENESS: HOW DO I START OVER AGAIN?

Here's what's happening:

✳✳1 MICHELLE: Michelle rises to the call. Her strength of character shines as she determines to change her behavior. Wisely, she doesn't wait until she feels like it or the circumstances are just right. She begins to work on behavioral changes immediately. Outwardly, things go well. Inwardly, she faces her toughest battle. A little voice asks why she allowed herself to do the things she did, tells her she'll slip again, and reminds her of all the fun she'll be missing. Starting all over again requires inside and outside changes.

◯1 ERIC: One of Eric's major tasks in becoming healthy was to forgive himself for the feelings, thoughts, and behaviors that were a part of his life for so long. Being forgiven and accepting forgiveness can be a challenging task.

Michelle and Eric seem to be doing well—but they still need to learn to forgive themselves. We'll continue their stories as soon as we've found out how that's done.

Forgiveness: How Do I Start Over Again?

Stained-glass windows can be incredibly beautiful, especially when you consider that they're nothing more than broken pieces of glass. Put together, however, by a skilled, artistic hand, the final result can be awesome. In the same way, our artistic heavenly Father can take the most shattered life and creatively put it together again. The potential for beauty boggles the mind.

In Japan enterprising physicians recreate hymens (the membrane around the opening of the vagina) so that Japanese brides can have a new "first" time. The symbolic breaking of a hymen, however, does not erase the emotional, social, and physical consequences of the first "first" time. Virginity can only be lost once.

Once a man asked Jesus how a person could be "born again" (John 3:4). Reentering a mother's womb seemed quite a trick! Jesus replied that the rebirth that counted was a spiritual one. Re-establishing virginity after having had sex does not involve a hymen, for the rebirth that occurs is spiritual. A transformation takes place, and a new stained-glass window is put together.

Forgiveness and new beginnings are instantly available to all who confess their sin and seriously ask for it (1 John 1:9). Jesus died to take the punishment for our wrongdoing. He did not die to remove all earthly consequences of our behavior or take away our feelings. Consequently, although true guilt is no longer a factor, learning to let go of shame and guilty feelings sometimes takes a long time.

Those who have been forgiven find a changed lifestyle possible because God, the artist, dedicates himself to redesigning a beautiful picture. "Therefore, prepare your minds for action; be self-controlled; set your hope fully on the grace to be given you when Jesus Christ is revealed. As obedient children, do not conform to the evil desires you had when you lived in ignorance" (1 Pet. 1:13–14).

Deciding not to have sex in a continuing relationship or determining not to succumb in new ones is not easy. Sex was

217

designed to feel good, and men and women were made to desire one another. God intends to help: "For it is God who works in you to will and to act according to his good purpose" (Phil. 2:13), and "No temptation has seized you except what is common to man. And God is faithful; he will not let you be tempted beyond what you can bear. But when you are tempted, he will also provide a way out so that you can stand up under it" (1 Cor. 10:13).

Making yourself accountable to a trustworthy person is a wise step in dealing with temptation. Restructuring old habits and rethinking what you do on dates, what movies you see, or what music you listen to, are just as important as establishing the level of physical intimacy you are comfortable with. It may mean a complete avoidance of any but the most platonic touching.

When you accept God's forgiveness and change your lifestyle to fit God's plan, you can enter a new relationship with a pure heart. The adage, "You can't start over again" is wrong. God takes the broken pieces of a life and makes something beautiful out of them: a new picture—unlimited possibility.

What happens next?

**1 MICHELLE (cont. from page 216)

As the small apartment rocked with the laughter of six teenage girls who had spent the evening playing "Pictionary," Caroline's mom had to remind the them for the third time to hold it down.

Heather was spread across the floor, propped up on her elbows. "I move we call Domino's," she said. "I need a jolt of pepperoni right now."

"You need a jolt of something, but I'm not sure it's pepperoni!" teased Betty. Her well-aimed pillow landed perfectly on Heather's enviable red curls. "What're you hungry for, Michelle?"

Michelle jumped slightly when she heard her name. Her mind had been wandering to six months before when being with a group of girls on a Friday night would have been decidedly "uncool." "Oh, me? Whatever you guys decide is fine with me."

Liz shook her head. "Remind me to give that girl a mind of

her own for Christmas, would ya?" she said. Everyone laughed, including Michelle.

Michelle knew these girls liked her. She had shared with Liz her anger and hurt over the boys' remarks—and her determination to change. Liz and this small group of girls had immediately responded to her need for friendship and support. She began going to church with them and enjoyed their occasional small gatherings like this. "OK, you win," Michelle surrendered. "How about a chocolate fudge sundae with whipped cream, nuts, and a maraschino cherry?"

The room came alive with groans.

Just then Caroline's mom came into the room with two giant bowls. "How about popcorn?" she asked, placing the bowls brimming with yummy-looking kernels on the floor between them. The aroma filled the room.

"I thought I smelled something good," Heather announced. "Maybe that's what started me thinking about food in the first place."

"Yeah, yeah, popcorn. That's what I meant I wanted!" Michelle replied. As she fell back on the floor in defeat, ten hands quickly held her down and began feeding her popcorn. And once again squeals and giggles filled the room.

The acceptance these girls showed Michelle mirrored the love and acceptance of Michelle's heavenly Father. She was a new person in Christ.

And she behaved like a new person—when she was with Heather and Caroline and the rest. But how would she behave on a date? Would she have the strength to break years of bad habits?

GO TO PAGE 54 AND LOOK FOR *⋅*1

O1 ERIC (cont. from page 216)

"Eric, it came! It came!" Anna didn't even wait until he got out of the car to hand him the letter.

"Well?" he teased.

She grabbed the letter back. "Well, you're the newest student at the seminary! You've been accepted for the fall class!" Anna punctuated the announcement with a little leap.

Arm in arm, they entered the house with Anna still waving the prized letter in the air.

Eric immediately proceeded to the nursery and scooped their baby out of the crib. "Come on, little one," he said. "Come celebrate with your mom and me. Today the Lord has done great things."

Snuggling together with his wife and baby on the sofa, Eric said a prayer of thanks. Then, looking up at his wife, he talked about his struggling times. "There were so many ups and downs," he recalled. "I knew the Lord could heal me, but I never imagined he would ever bless me this much!"

"Remember the first time Pastor Davidson suggested you might have a ministry with others who struggle as you did?" Anna asked.

Eric nodded. "I laughed," he admitted.

"Well," she said, brandishing the letter above her head, "this is no laughing matter, and neither is our celebration dinner."

Anna disappeared into the kitchen, and Eric was left holding his small, peacefully sleeping son. Although the baby hadn't found the celebration exciting enough to stay awake for, Eric was a joyful man.

IF YOU WANT TO EXPLORE OTHER CHOICES ERIC MIGHT HAVE MADE, RETURN TO PAGE 18 OR 196.